*MILNER CRAFT SERIES*

# Metric Quiltmaking

MARGARET ROLFE
WITH BERYL HODGES AND JUDY TURNER

SALLY MILNER PUBLISHING

First published in 1993 by
Sally Milner Publishing Pty Ltd
558 Darling Street
Rozelle NSW 2039
Australia

© Margaret Rolfe, 1993

Design by Gatya Kelly, Dorie Order
Photography by Michael Pugh
Typeset in Australia by Character Typesetting
Printed in Australia by Impact Printing, Melbourne

National Library of Australia
Cataloguing-in-Publication data:

Rolfe, Margaret.
  Metric quiltmaking.

  ISBN 1 86351 116 4.

  1. Quilting. 2. Quilts. I. Title. (Series : Milner craft series).

746.97

All rights reserved. No part of this publication may be reproduced, stored in a retrieval system or transmitted in any form or by any means, electronic, mechanical, photocopying, recording or otherwise, without prior written permission of the copyright owners and publishers.

# CONTENTS

| | |
|---|---|
| A Word from the Author | |
| Metric Versus Imperial: The Problem in Patchwork | 1 |
| Understanding the Terms of Quiltmaking | 4 |
| Equipment and Materials | 7 |
| Using your Rotary Cutter | 12 |
| Sewing | 33 |
| Quilt Construction | 43 |
| Designing a Quilt | 63 |
| Patchwork Shapes and Block Designs | 77 |
| Quilt Projects | 105 |
|    Summer Roses | 105 |
|    Country Checks | 109 |
|    Bear's Paw | 111 |
|    Lady of the Lake | 114 |
|    Marching Geese | 117 |
|    Sailing Ships | 120 |
|    Vibrant Stars | 123 |
|    Ohio Star | 126 |
| Converting Imperial Measurements to Metric | 129 |
| Index | 132 |

# A WORD FROM THE AUTHOR

Every book must justify its existence, at the very least if only to the trees which provide the paper. I have vowed that, if I am to continue to write books, each one must give the reader something new, something they won't find in any other book. I hope you will think this book achieves my purpose, as it not only brings you instructions on how to make quilts using metric measurements (a long overdue area, may I say), but it also gives you a basic handbook on modern-day quilting methods. The women of today, with their multi-faceted, busy lives, need techniques that produce results — and produce them fast. I hope you will be delighted with the quick and easy methods described here, leaving you with time to concentrate on the creative aspects of quiltmaking.

I have written this book in conjunction with Beryl Hodges and Judy Turner, two of Australia's outstanding quilt teachers and quiltmakers. I have very much appreciated their input, based on their wealth of experience through both teaching and quiltmaking. In the process of writing about the techniques, we found we often differed about the way we liked to do things. The finished results were the same — great quilts — but our methods varied somewhat here and there. For instance, Beryl and I are happy to pick up the fabric after it has been squared up, and to turn it around ready for the next cut. Judy doesn't like to do this. She prefers to turn the fabric around by leaving it on the mat and then turning around the whole cutting mat. So, often in the book you will find we have presented some alternative methods, and it is up to you to choose the one with which you are most comfortable. This may seem like just a little point, but it illustrates something important I have long held about quiltmaking: there are no rules — if it works for you, then it is right to do.

We present here the combination and culmination of all our experience. We hope this will help you — but feel free to do things your own way!

**Margaret Rolfe**

# METRIC VERSUS IMPERIAL:
## THE PROBLEM IN PATCHWORK

Quiltmaking, especially quiltmaking using modern techniques, has come to be associated with imperial measurements. There are two reasons for this. The first is that most of the quilt books, equipment and materials come from the United States of America, where quiltmaking has become very popular since the Bicentennial in 1976, and where the imperial measuring system is still used. The second is simply that imperial measurements have been particularly well suited to quiltmaking. The first reason concerns history, but the second leads us to the reason this book needed to be written. It is quite a long story, which I shall now relate.

In the early days, quiltmaking was done by hand. Templates were cut, then the pieces of fabric were marked and sewn together with the stitching following the marked sewing line. In the middle of the last century, the sewing machine was invented and many women began doing patchwork by machine. People realised that in order to machine sew many simple patchwork patterns, it was easier to cut out the patches with the seam allowance included. So, instead of following a marked sewing line, you just lined up the cut edge of the fabric with either the sewing foot of the machine, or a marked line on the plate of the sewing machine. The pieces of fabric were still marked, but the marking was done on the cutting line, so the cut-out shape included the seam allowance. The generally chosen (though not universal) size for the seam allowance for machine piecing was ¼" (a quarter-inch). So, techniques for hand or machine sewing patchwork blocks diverged. For hand sewing, marking was done on the sewing line; for machine sewing, marking was done on the cutting line.

With the quilt revival in the 1970s and '80s, a revolution took place. New quiltmaking tools were invented, notably the rotary cutter and its companion, the wide, clear plastic ruler. Fabric cutting became quick and easy, and marking the fabric became unnecessary for the simple traditional patchwork shapes of the square, rectangle and triangle.

By adopting a standard ¼" seam allowance, squares and rectangles could be cut just ½" larger than the finished size. Triangles could be made by first cutting squares, then recutting the squares either once across the diagonal to make half-square triangles, or twice across to make quarter-square triangles. Formulae were determined to make the precise size of these squares for cutting triangles. For the half-square triangle, you cut a square ⅞" larger than the finished size, then cut once through the diagonal; for the quarter-square triangle, you cut a square 1¼" larger than the finished size, then cut across both diagonals. All these measurements depended on both cutting and sewing an accurate ¼" seam allowance.

# METRIC QUILTMAKING

It was in the conversion of the ¼" seam allowance that metric quiltmaking came unstuck. The ¼" seam was converted into a 6 mm (0.6 cm) metric seam allowance. But when 6 mm is doubled, it becomes 12 mm or 1.2 cm. This is a most inconvenient figure and metric quiltmaking became a non-issue. Heaven knows how you went on to cut triangles, as no one bothered to try. The system was not even very useful for cutting simple squares and rectangles.

This book aims to present the answer to the problem: make the seam allowance 0.75 cm. With the 0.75 cm seam allowance, all the measurements become straightforward and simple. Twice 0.75 cm becomes 1.5 cm — the size needed for the seam allowances on squares and rectangles. For half-square triangles, add 2.5 cm. To cut quarter-square triangles, add 3.5 cm. It is simple and easy to remember: 1.5 cm, 2.5 cm, and 3.5 cm!

Now, metric measurements can be used for all quiltmaking, and imperial measurements can be converted to metric measurements when you wish to make quilts using the new quick-cutting techniques. No longer do we need to switch awkwardly from one system to the other the way we do when we buy fabric by the metre, only to cut it up into yards, feet and inches.

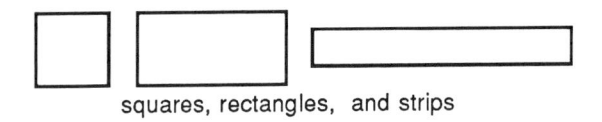

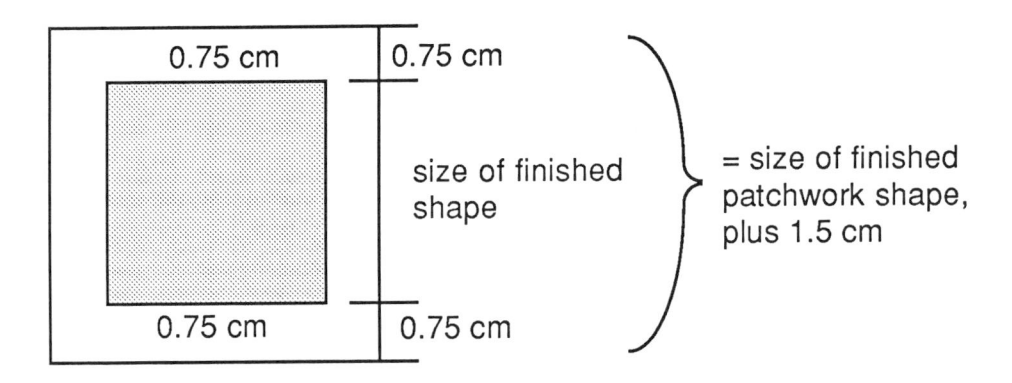

squares, rectangles, and strips

0.75 cm | 0.75 cm

size of finished shape   } = size of finished patchwork shape, plus 1.5 cm

0.75 cm | 0.75 cm

# METRIC VERSUS IMPERIAL

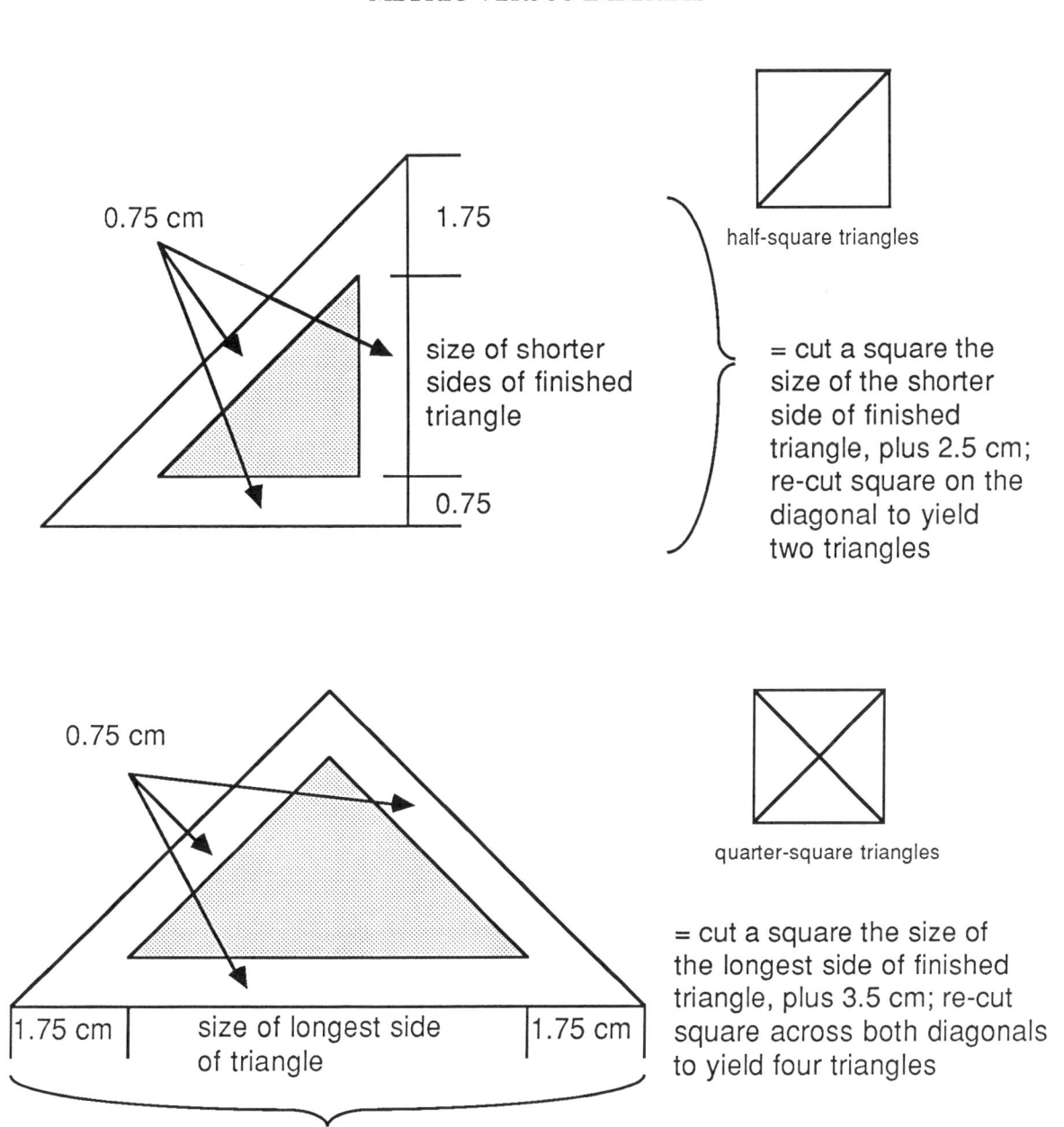

0.75 cm

1.75

size of shorter sides of finished triangle

0.75

half-square triangles

= cut a square the size of the shorter side of finished triangle, plus 2.5 cm; re-cut square on the diagonal to yield two triangles

0.75 cm

1.75 cm

size of longest side of triangle

1.75 cm

quarter-square triangles

= cut a square the size of the longest side of finished triangle, plus 3.5 cm; re-cut square across both diagonals to yield four triangles

Very importantly, we can now teach our children to make quilts without first having to teach them imperial measurements. A whole generation has grown up with imperial measurements and is happy to keep on using them. But we don't want our craft to die with us because we're using what has become an outmoded measuring system. Quiltmaking is a joy and a pleasure. By working metrically and using the latest equipment and techniques, we ensure future generations equal joy and pleasure.

# UNDERSTANDING THE TERMS OF QUILTMAKING

Like most crafts, quiltmaking has a vocabulary of its own.

**A quilt** consists of three layers:
1. The quilt top — where the patchwork pattern will be.
2. The batting — the padded layer in the middle.
3. The backing — the fabric at the back of the quilt.

**Quilting:** The stitching which holds these three layers together; it can be done by hand or machine.

**Piecing:** The process by which the pieces of fabric in patchwork are sewn together by seaming them side by side. (In contrast, **appliqué** is a process in which a piece, or pieces, of fabric are sewn on top of another piece of fabric.)

**Finished size:** The measurement of a patchwork piece, a block or a quilt top without seam allowances being included.

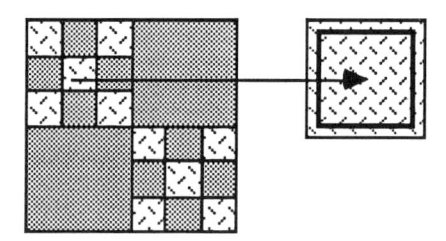

Finished size refers to the size of the finished shape in the patchwork, without seam allowances added.

# UNDERSTANDING THE TERMS OF QUILTMAKING

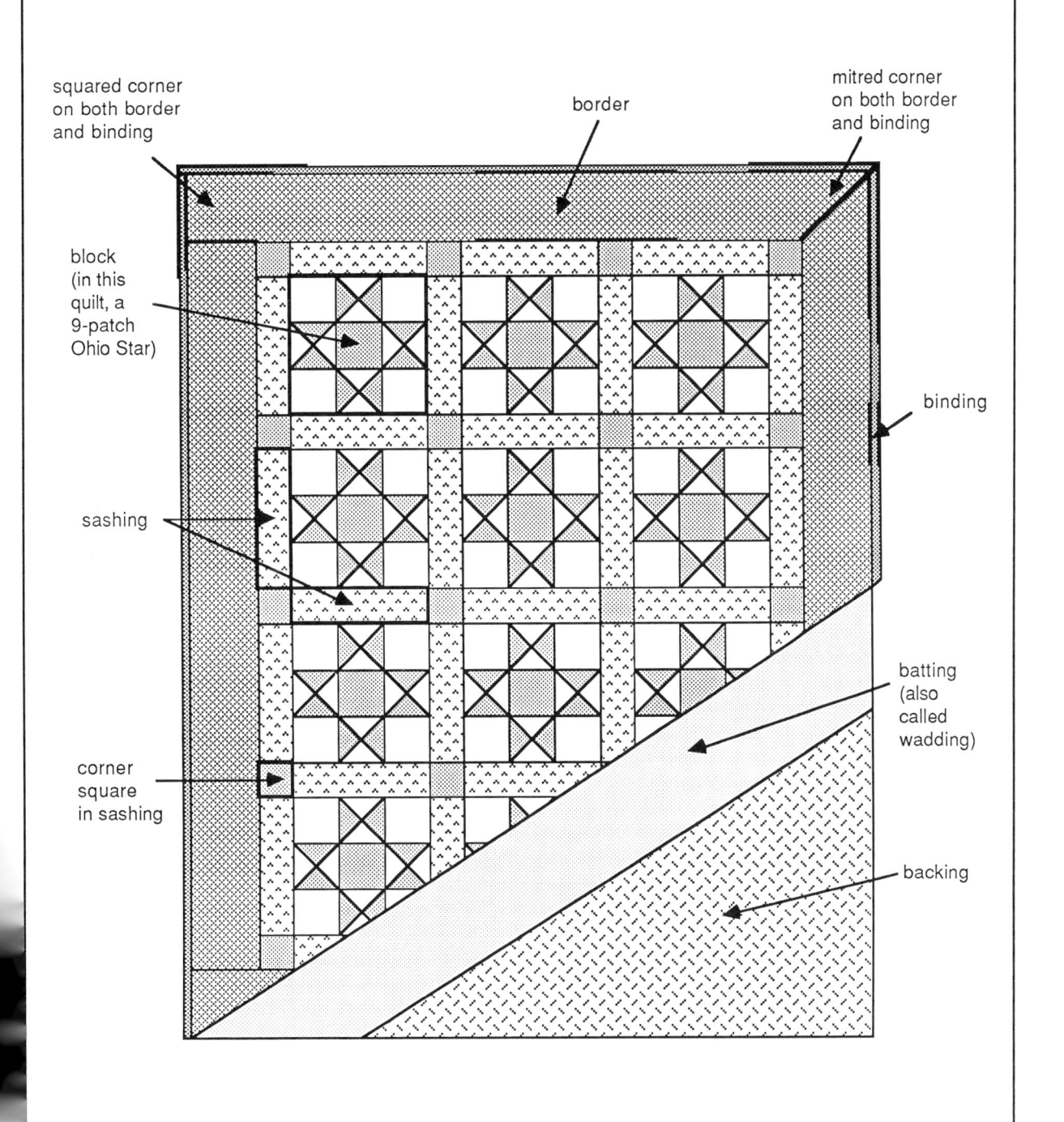

- squared corner on both border and binding
- border
- mitred corner on both border and binding
- block (in this quilt, a 9-patch Ohio Star)
- binding
- sashing
- batting (also called wadding)
- corner square in sashing
- backing

Understanding a Quilt

METRIC QUILTMAKING

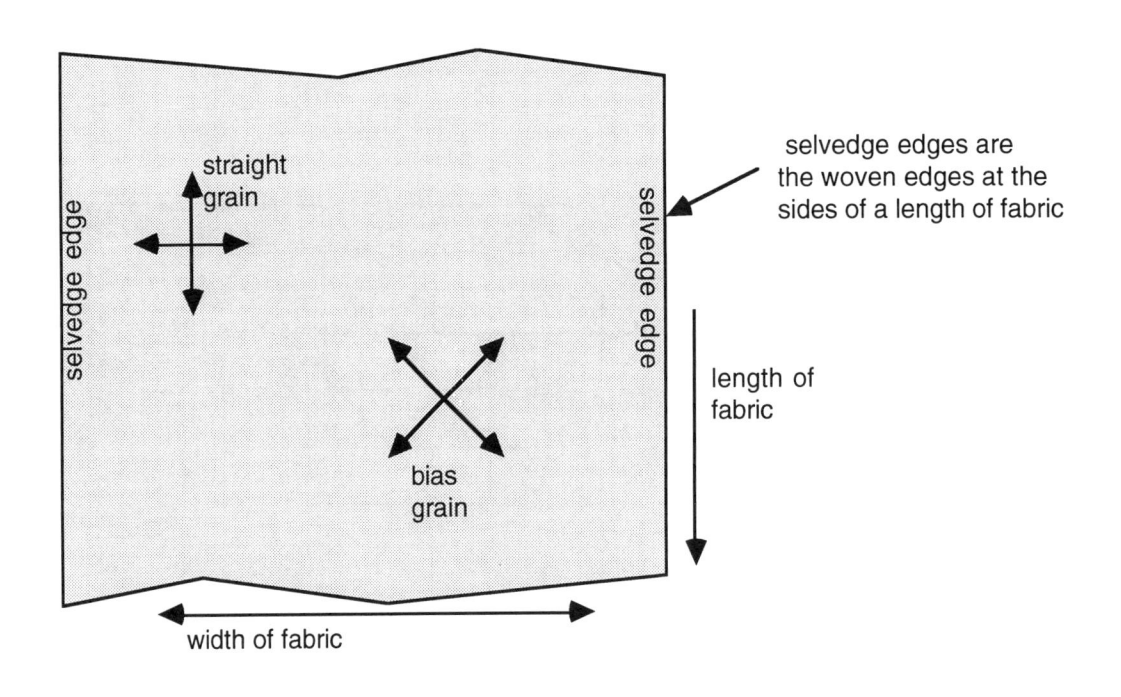

- selvedge edges are the woven edges at the sides of a length of fabric
- selvedge edge
- straight grain
- bias grain
- length of fabric
- width of fabric

straight grain follows the direction of the threads on the fabric

Understanding fabric and fabric grain

# EQUIPMENT AND MATERIALS

#### EQUIPMENT

SEWING MACHINE

Your sewing machine is the most important tool for quiltmaking. It doesn't have to do fancy stitches, because only straight stitching is required for both piecing and quilting. Keep your machine cleaned and well oiled, and have a spare packet of needles on hand.

If you plan to machine quilt, a walking foot helps keep the layers moving smoothly through the machine without shifting. Some models of machine have a walking foot built in, but for others, this can be purchased as an extra attachment.

IRON

An iron is used constantly for machine-sewn patchwork, because each seam is pressed after sewing. Set up the iron as near to your sewing as possible. A small ironing board which sits on a table top is useful. Or you may like to make yourself a simple board by covering a small piece of light pineboard with several layers of fabric.

ROTARY CUTTER AND MAT

The rotary cutter has revolutionised quiltmaking, making cutting quick, accurate and simple. Keep your cutter for fabric only, and renew the blade as soon as it stops cutting smoothly. The correct sensation for cutting is that you feel you are cutting soft butter rather than bread. The blade on the rotary cutter is extremely sharp, but is protected by a guard which you click or push out of place when you are using the ruler. Always remember to put the guard back in place immediately after use, so that the cutter is never left with the blade unprotected.

A mat is essential to go with the cutter, and a large one is much better than small. If possible, choose one with a grid printed on it, because the lines assist you in measuring. It doesn't matter if the grid on the mat is not in metric measurements; no matter what the measurements are, the grid still gives give you parallel lines in both directions and right angles.

# METRIC QUILTMAKING

Although a cutter and mat represent a sizeable investment, you'll find that the time they save will make them well worth the cost.

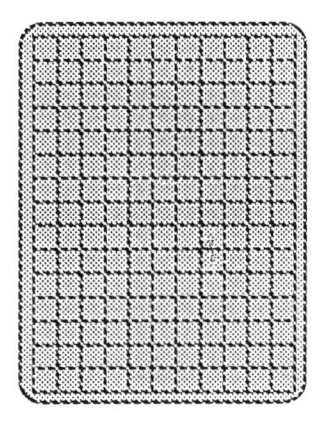

*cutting mat with grid marked*

*long rectangular ruler*

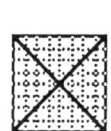

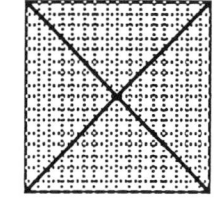

*square rulers*

## QUILTING RULERS

To make quilts using metric measurements, metric quilting rulers are essential. The rulers should be marked so that half-centimetre intervals are clear. The Australian-made Metric Quilting Rules are ideal. The rulers should also have clearly marked diagonal lines (45° angle), enabling you to cut shapes on the bias grain.

Ideally, have three different rulers:

1. Long rectangular ruler. The most important ruler, it is used mainly to cut strips but is also suitable for all other shapes.

2. Small square ruler. This is easier to manage than the large ruler when you are recutting strips into small squares and triangles.

3. Large square ruler. Useful for cutting large squares and triangles, it is also suitable for trimming the edges of blocks once they are sewn.

## SCISSORS

Although most cutting will be done using the rotary cutter, you also need scissors to cut batting and fabric. Keep a pair of thread snips next to your sewing machine as well, to cut thread ends.

# EQUIPMENT AND MATERIALS

SEAM RIPPER
Keep one of these close by your machine for those occasions when you need to unpick some sewing.

PINS
Quick quiltmaking techniques described in this book need a minimum of pinning, but some pinning will be necessary at times. Choose pins with berry-heads; they are kind to fingers and easy to find when dropped.

Several hundred small safety pins (about 3 cm in length) are essential to pin the layers together in preparation for machine quilting. These pins can sometimes be obtained in bulk from dry cleaners.

NEEDLES
For hand quilting, you need a 'between' needle — a short, small-eyed needle used especially in quilting. It comes in various sizes, but most people choose an 8 or 9. You'll need a larger size if using a thicker thread.

For hand-finishing the binding on a quilt or appliqué, choose any size needle you feel comfortable in using.

QUILTING HOOP OR FRAME
If you are hand quilting, you need either a quilting hoop or a frame to keep the layers in place while stitching. A hoop is convenient and inexpensive, and can be turned easily to allow you to quilt in any direction. Choose a size of hoop that suits your arm length — around 35 cm in diameter is a popular size. You should be able to reach the centre of the hoop comfortably without stretching. The depth of the hoop should be about 2.5 cm.

A full-size quilting frame needs space, but enables more than one person to quilt at a time.

THIMBLES
When hand quilting, you need to protect your fingers with one or more thimbles. Choose a size that fits your finger, neither so tight that it is uncomfortable, nor so loose that it falls off. A thimble is worn on the third finger of your sewing hand, and is used to push the needle through the layers of the quilt. A second thimble or other kind of finger protector is worn on the second or third finger of

the hand underneath the quilt, to protect it from being grazed by the needle as you guide it back up through the layers of the quilt.

### MASKING TAPE
Masking tape is useful for marking lines on your quilting rulers so that you don't have to look for the right line each time you cut. It also can be used to mark lines for hand quilting.

### DRESSMAKER'S CHALK
Quilting lines, especially lines for machine quilting, can be marked with dressmaker's chalk. This is sold in little blocks, in pencil form and in chalk markers which dispense powdered chalk. The markers are the most convenient because they draw a thin line.

### PENCIL
Good quality, sharp HB pencils are used to mark quilts for hand quilting.

### METRE RULER
A metre ruler is used to mark long quilting lines across a quilt. These can be bought cheaply at hardware stores. Alternatively, use a long, smooth piece of hardwood.

### PIN-BOARD OR FLANNELETTE SHEET
Professional quilters have large pin-boards covered in white felt on which to put their quilts during construction in order to check the colour and design. Cheaper, but effective, is a plain-coloured flannelette sheet which you can pin up when you need it. While you will need to pin the patchwork blocks or pieces to the sheet, you'll find that the fluffy pile on the flannelette will help the patchwork adhere smoothly (so, a worn or ordinary sheet is not as satisfactory as a new flannelette one).

Having some way of pinning up your work is especially important when you are making scrap quilts. You need to be able to balance the tonal values and colours, and only by pinning up the piece and standing back, can you see clearly how well the quilt is working.

# EQUIPMENT AND MATERIALS

## Materials

### FABRIC

Pure cotton fabrics are the best and easiest to use in quiltmaking. They cut crisply, iron flat and sew without stretching. There are myriads of wonderful patterned and plain fabrics available especially for quilting, but any pure cotton dress or curtain fabric can be used. Sometimes you may find that a particular colour or pattern you need is only available in a blend or polyester fabric. As colour is more important than anything else, go ahead and use it, but bear in mind that it will not behave as well as pure cotton. For suggestions on choosing colours and prints for your quilts, see p. 72.

Wash and press all your fabrics before use. It is good to get into the habit of washing and pressing fabrics immediately after purchase so they are ready to sew when inspiration strikes.

### BATTING

Many types of batting are available; choice is dependent on personal preference. Polyester batting (in various thicknesses), offers a nice loft, is usually soft to quilt through and washes beautifully. Cotton batting gives quilts a traditional look, but it needs closer quilting and may not have as much loft as polyester. Woollen batting offers warmth and softness and is less flammable than other fibres. However, woollen fibres are prone to "beard" through the patchwork, so it is better not to use a light-coloured wool batting under dark fabrics.

Choose a thinner batting for machine quilting; the less bulk you have to manoeuvre through the machine, the easier quilting will be.

### THREAD

For machine piecing, use dressmaking or overlocking thread. White or cream thread can be used for most patchwork, but use black or another dark thread if you are working with predominantly dark fabrics.

For machine quilting, choose either a transparent monofilament thread which blends with all colours, or, match the thread to the predominant colour. For the bobbin thread, match the colour to the backing fabric. Do not use monofilament thread in the bobbin.

For hand quilting, use quilting thread. This comes in many colours, so don't feel limited to white, cream or black.

# USING YOUR ROTARY CUTTER

The rotary cutter is a twentieth-century revolutionary tool for quick quiltmaking. But, like all tools, it must be used with care and precision. It cannot be stressed enough that your rotary cutter has a **very sharp** blade. It cuts fabric cleanly and easily; if it cuts your finger, it will do so with equal ease, but the results will certainly not be clean.

SAFETY RULES
1. **Always close your rotary cutter after every use**. Never leave your cutter lying around with its blade open. Some types of rotary cutter have a safety element built in, so that the blade comes out of its sheath only as you push down to use it. But if you have the type of cutter that has to have the guard pulled back out of the way before use, train yourself automatically to flick the blade guard in place whenever you put the cutter down. Make it a habit to flick the guard away just before you begin to cut and to flick it back immediately after the cut is finished.

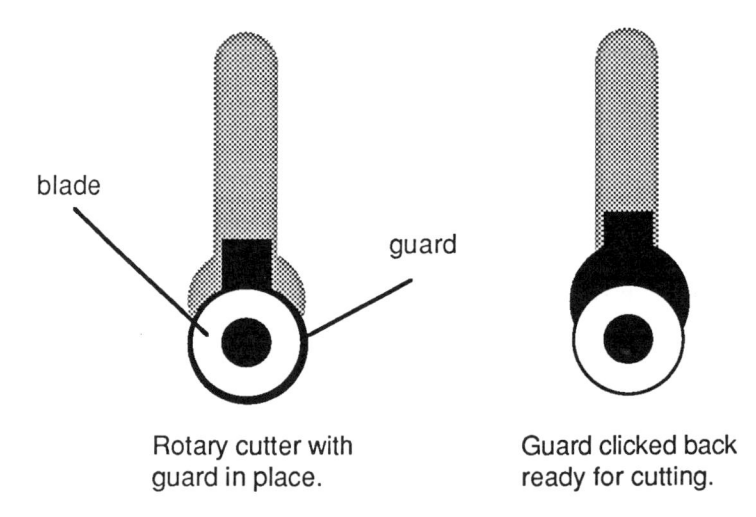

The rotary cutter

Rotary cutter with guard in place.

Guard clicked back ready for cutting.

2. **Position your fingers on the quilting ruler so that they are never in line with the blade.** Place your hand holding the ruler so that your fingers press down firmly on top of it. Extend one or two fingers out over the edge away from the cutter, to hold the ruler in place and to stop it slipping. Never extend any of your fingers on the cutting side — always extend them over the opposite side.

## USING YOUR ROTARY CUTTER

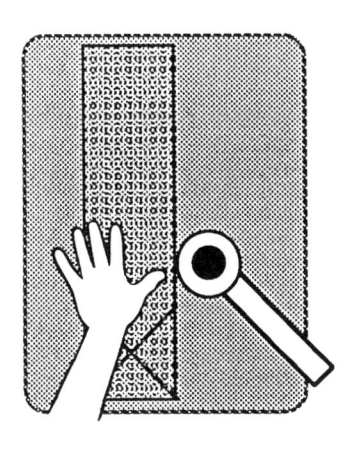

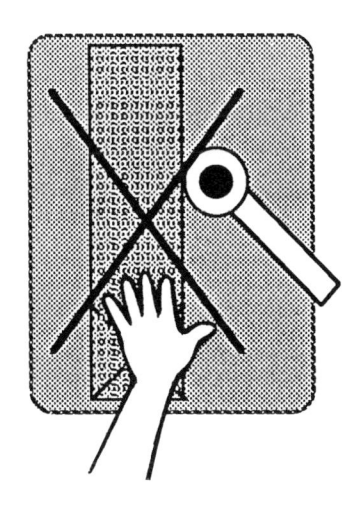

3. **Always cut away from yourself.**

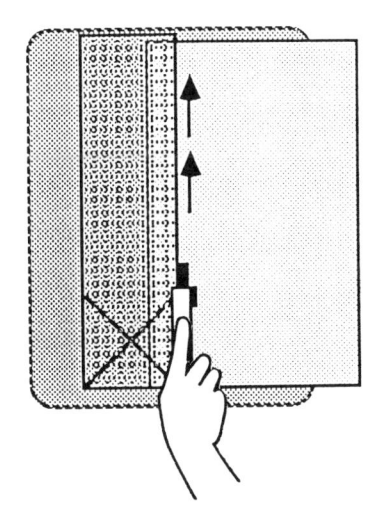

CUTTING IN COMFORT

It is important to make your rotary cutting as comfortable as possible, so pay some attention to how you set yourself up to work.

1. Find the height which suits you best. Most people find that they need to stand while using the rotary cutter, especially when cutting out long strips. While a table is the most commonly used base for rotary cutting, the height is actually too low for many. Consider using your kitchen bench, especially if you have a lot of cutting to do. Try out the possibilities to find what suits you best. You may like to vary your position. Try standing to cut long strips, but

sitting to cut smaller ones, perhaps with some cushions added to your chair to increase your height.

2. Position the cutting mat. While most people automatically place the cutting mat so that it is a horizontal rectangle in front of them, generally it is better to place the mat in a position to take advantage of its maximum length to cut long strips.

### LOOKING AFTER YOUR BODY

When you are doing a lot of rotary cutting, be conscious of the time and take frequent breaks. Walk around and swing your arms, flex your fingers, and make your back concave by pushing out your chest and pulling back your shoulders. You'd be surprised how much force you are using on both the cutter and the ruler, so give your body a chance to relax and loosen up from time to time.

### ARRANGING THE FABRIC READY FOR CUTTING

There are three ways in which you can arrange the fabric ready for cutting. The choice depends on the size of the fabric you are working on, and whether you want to cut it lengthwise or widthwise. For larger pieces of fabric, you'll need to make one or more folds to make it fit on top of your mat.

### FOLDING THE FABRIC

Before larger pieces of fabric can be cut, they must first be folded. It is important to follow the proper procedure, because, if your fabric is folded correctly to begin with, cuts will be how they ought to be — straight and on-grain. Generally you are aiming to have the fold on the grain of the fabric (unless you are cutting bias strips, in which case the fold is on the bias).

### THREE WAYS OF ARRANGING THE FABRIC

1. For cutting across the width of the fabric

This is the most common way of cutting strips, especially as fabric is often bought in short 20—30 cm lengths just for patchwork. Fabric is generally 112 cm wide, so it must be cut folded in half to fit on your mat, with your ruler extended a little at each end.

Fold the fabric down the centre, **on the grain**. As you do this, the selvedge edges should roughly meet, but remember that folding on the straight grain of the fabric is more important than making the selvedges meet exactly. Often, fabric is crookedly cut and the selvedges are not straight, making it difficult to line them up. Stand up to make the fold. Hold the fabric out in front of you, so that you can clearly see the grain. The fold will be horizontal, and your hands either side of it. Pinch the fold in between your fingers, adjusting the fabric between your fingertips until the fold is exactly on the grain.

## USING YOUR ROTARY CUTTER

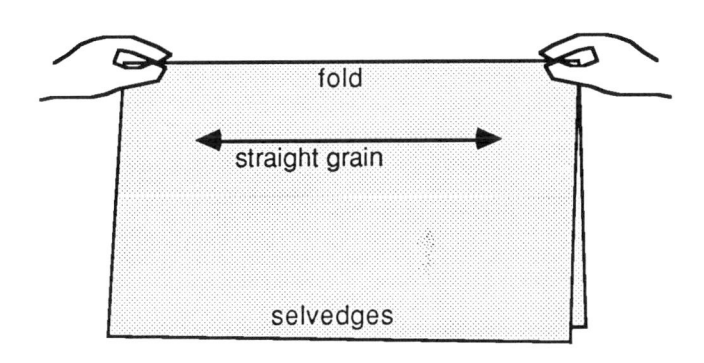

Give the fabric a little shake so that it falls smooth and flat. Lay it out on your cutting board, the fold nearest to you so that you can look directly down onto it. It is important to be able to see the fold when you are lining it up with the bottom edge of the ruler. If you have a mat with a grid marked on it, you'll find it useful to match the fold with one of the horizontal lines on the grid.

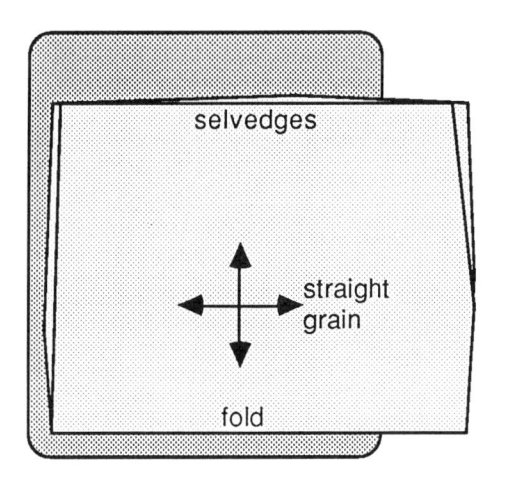

Arranging the fabric for cutting strips across the fabric width

### 2. For cutting down the length of the fabric

You will need to cut down the length of the fabric to create long strips for sashing or borders. Any fabric you even *think* you may want to use for sashing or borders should be cut down its length; it's very irritating to find you have the right fabric for a border, but that it is several centimetres too short because you have taken some widthways strips off it.

# METRIC QUILTMAKING

Fold the fabric across its width, making enough folds so that the fabric will fit on the mat. Remember that the folds should be kept on grain and the selvedge edges should be aligned. Make as few folds as possible, but make the fabric into a neat package that will fit on your mat and not extend beyond the length of your ruler.

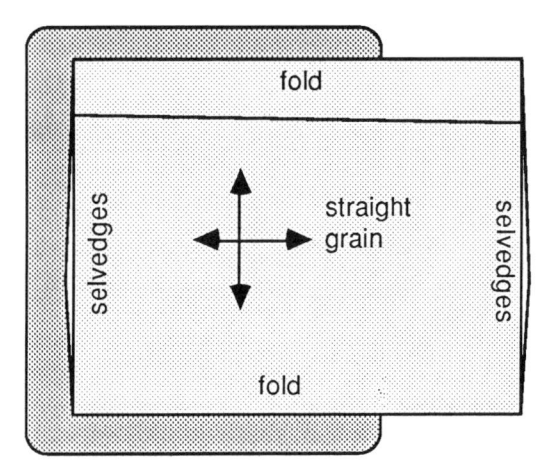

Arranging the fabric for cutting strips down the fabric length

3. For cutting small and irregular-shaped pieces
Often you will be cutting small and odd-shaped pieces of fabric. Arrange the fabric so that the **grain** is horizontal and vertical in front of you.

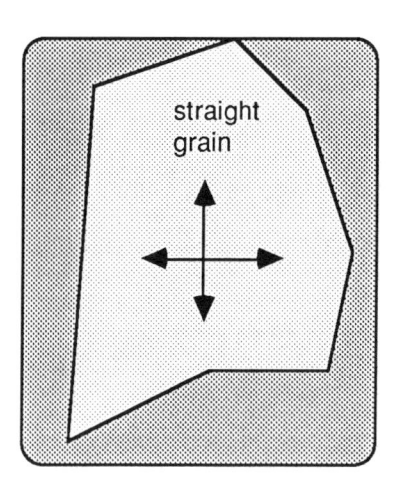

Arranging the fabric for small odd shaped pieces of fabric

# USING YOUR ROTARY CUTTER

## USING THE RULER

Quilting rulers are a little different from other rulers in that they not only measure length (i.e. they have markings which go down the length of the ruler), they also measure width (i.e. they have markings which go across its width). Generally, it is these widthways measurements which you will be using to measure and cut your patchwork shapes. The length of the ruler is used as an edge for you to run the cutter along, as well as for making measurements.

To measure width, the ruler is placed so that one of its widthways markings lines up with a straight edge of the fabric. A cut is then made down the length of the ruler, giving a strip in the width chosen. Note that, to be used accurately, the ruler must always be placed on top of a straight edge.

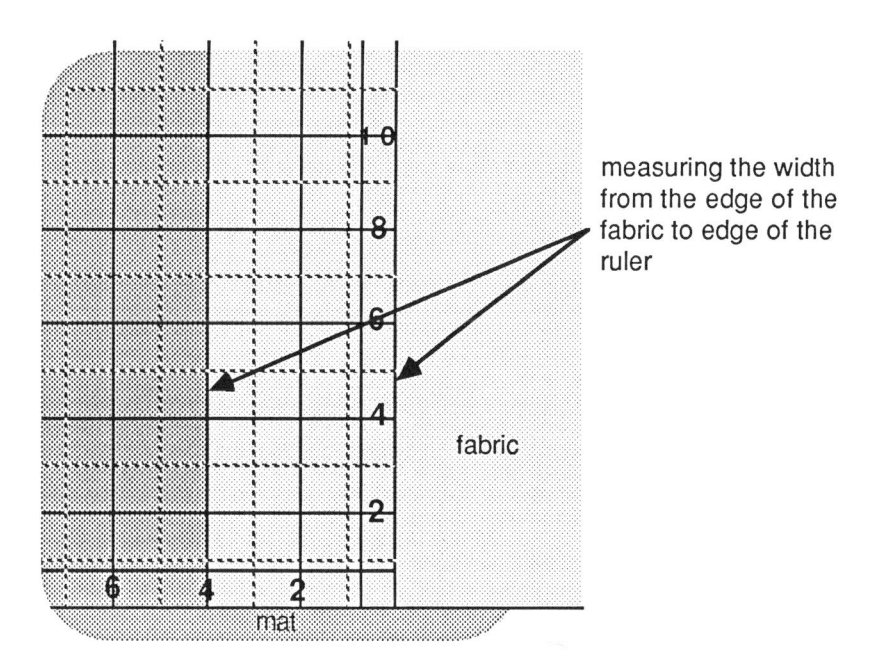

measuring the width from the edge of the fabric to edge of the ruler

POSITIONING THE RULER
1. Carefully place the ruler in its exact position, always checking along its length to see that it is precisely where you want it to be in relation to the cut you are making.
2. Spread your hand across the ruler, positioning one or two of your fingers off the edge of the ruler on the side **away** from the cutter. This will help prevent the ruler moving sideways.
3. Press down firmly on the ruler, keeping an even pressure on it from the beginning to the end of the cut.
4. On a long cut, you may find that you have to 'walk' your hand along the ruler. Keep pressing down firmly all the while, so the ruler does not move. Keep movements such as these to a minimum. Any movement increases the likelihood of the ruler slipping and making the cut inaccurate.

### USING THE ROTARY CUTTER

1. Flick the guard out of place just before you begin to cut.
2. Hold the cutter firmly in your hand with the blade vertical. The cutting edge of the blade should be exactly alongside the ruler. Begin at the edge of the fabric which is closest to you.
3. Cut smoothly down the length of the ruler, **always cutting away from yourself**.
4. After each cut, flick the guard back into place.

### SQUARING UP THE FABRIC

The first step in rotary cutting is to square up the fabric so that you have a perfectly straight edge on which to place your ruler for subsequent cuts. If this first cut is precise and accurate, all the rest of your cutting will be, too. The aim is not only to have the edge straight, but also to have the cut on-grain, (hence the importance of having any folds on the grain).

Note that, before strips are cut into squares or rectangles, they also need to have their ends squared up, employing one of the methods given below. You may use the small square ruler if you are only working on one strip.

THREE METHODS OF SQUARING UP THE FABRIC

1. Using two rulers

The advantage of this method is that when you have squared up the fabric, it is correctly in place for your next and subsequent cuts.

   a) Place your fabric on the cutting mat, the bulk of the fabric on the side of your dominant hand. For right-handed people, the bulk will be to your right and the edge you will be cutting to the left. If the fabric is folded, the fold should be just in front of you.

   b) Take a square quilting ruler and place it on top of the fabric fold, near to the edge of the fabric. Either match an edge of the ruler to the horizontal grain of the fabric, or, match an edge of the ruler exactly with the fold (which should be on the grain line). If there is a fold, one edge of the square ruler should now form an exact right-angle to this fold.

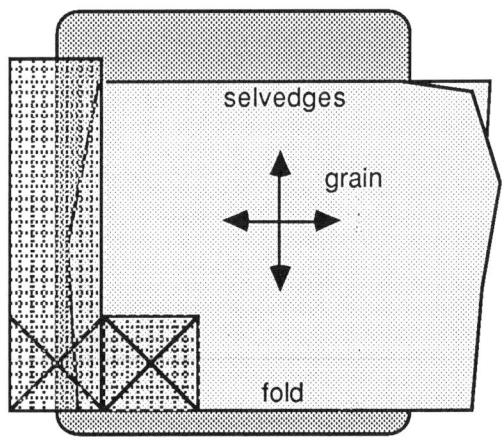

Squaring up the fabric with two rulers

## USING YOUR ROTARY CUTTER

c) Take the long rectangular ruler and place it exactly next to your square ruler. The long rectangular ruler now is making a right-angle to the horizontal grain (or fold).

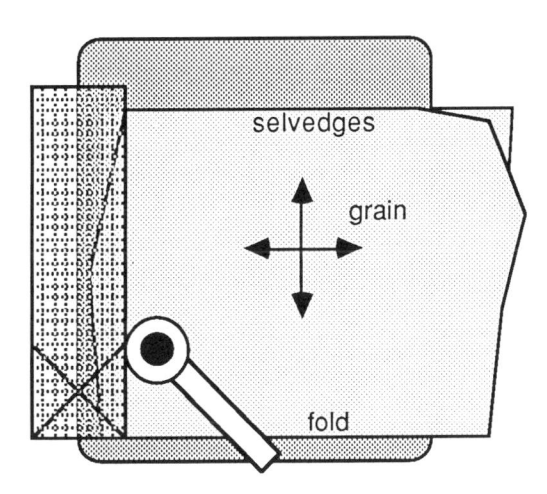

d) Pressing firmly down on the long ruler, take away the square ruler and cut along the edge of the rectangular ruler.

e) You are now ready to make your next cut, without having to move the fabric.

Squaring up the fabric with one ruler

### 2. Using one long rectangular ruler

The disadvantage of this method is that when you have squared up the fabric, it will be opposite to the way you need it for the next cut. The fabric must be turned around before making a second cut.

a) Place fabric on the mat so that the bulk of it is away from your dominant hand. For right-handed people, this will mean that the bulk is on the left side and the edge you will be cutting is on the right.

b) Place the long ruler on top of the fabric near to the edge that is to be cut. Place the length of the ruler exactly on top of the vertical grain of the fabric. If the fabric is folded, align the bottom of the ruler with the fold exactly, so that the cut will be at a right-angle to the fold.

c) Cut along the edge of the ruler, while holding the ruler firmly in place.

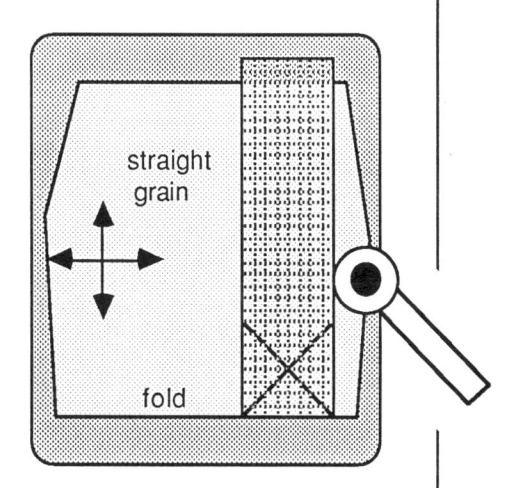

d) To make the next cut, the fabric must be around the opposite way so that the bulk of it is on the side of your dominant hand (right side for right-handers). There are several possible ways of doing this:

- You can pick up the fabric and turn it around. The edge you will be cutting next should now be away from your dominant hand. If you are turning folded fabric, it must be very carefully handled so as not to disturb the cut edges. Pick up the fabric along the cut edges, using both hands and pinching the cut edges between your fingers so that they remain neatly together. Flip the fabric over, then check that all the cut edges remain aligned; make any necessary adjustments.

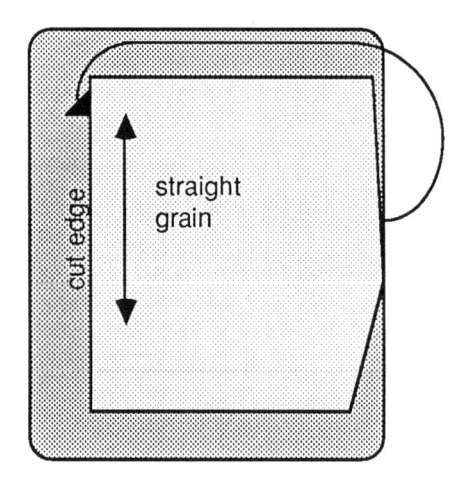

- Turn the whole mat around, leaving the fabric folded on top of it and being careful that the fabric is not disturbed in the process.

- Do the remaining cuts from the opposite side of the mat. This is possible if you are cutting with the mat on a bench, for instance. You can make the first squaring cut from one side of the mat, then go around to the other side to make further cuts.

3. Using the grid markings on the cutting mat

This method leaves the fabric on the side needed for subsequent cuts, but you must use a mat with a marked grid.

a) Lay the fabric so that the horizontal grain matches a horizontal line on your mat. If the fabric is folded, match the fold with a horizontal line on the mat. The bulk of the fabric must be on the same side as your dominant hand (right side for right-handers).

b) Match the vertical line on the mat with the edge of your ruler; cut.

## USING YOUR ROTARY CUTTER

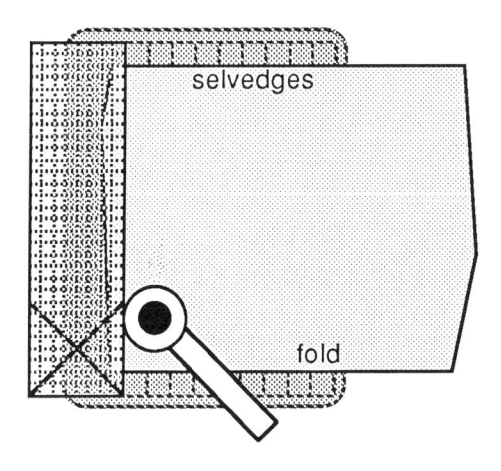

### CHECKING ACCURACY
If you have folded the fabric with care and lined up your rulers exactly with the fold line, your cutting should be at exactly 90° (i.e. at a right-angle) to the fold. You can check the accuracy of your first cut by opening out your fabric. You should see a perfectly straight line, not an angled edge. If there is any angle, refold the fabric carefully and begin again. To avoid repeated folding, practise making the first cut accurately so that continual checking is not necessary. With experience of folding and cutting on the grain, you'll find your cutting will become accurate. The main principle to remember is that, if there is a fold, the cut must be at an exact right angle (90°) to it.

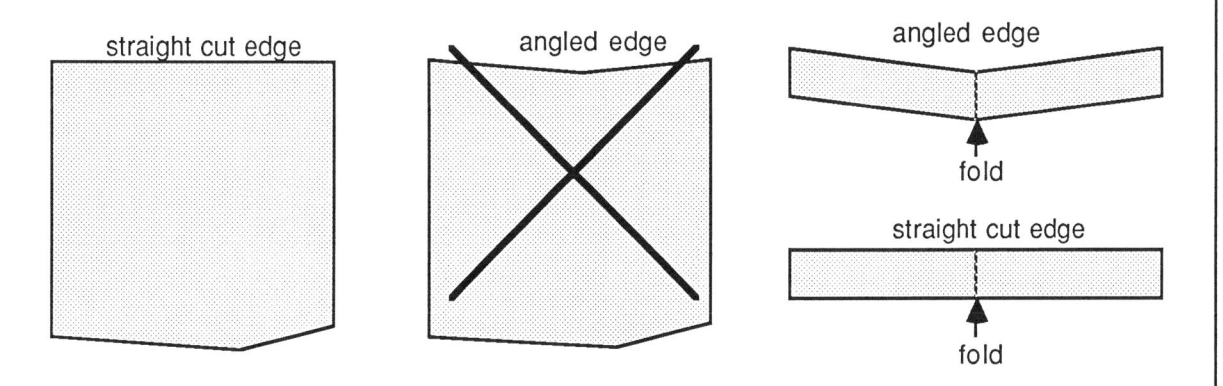

### CUTTING STRIPS
Cutting strips is the most fundamental process of all the rotary cutting techniques. Before most other shapes are cut, the fabric must be cut into strips. These can be cut on the straight grain or the bias of the fabric.

## CUTTING STRAIGHT-GRAIN STRIPS

1. Place your fabric so that its bulk is on the same side as your dominant hand, and your already-cut straight edge is on the other side. For right-handed people, the bulk will be on the right, the cut edge on the left. If the fabric is folded, the fold should be nearest to you, and should be on the grain of the fabric.

2. Move your ruler carefully on top of the fabric, lining up the cut edge with a line of the ruler that will give you the width you want. This must be done precisely; the strip must be exactly the same width throughout its whole length.

3. Cut along the length of the ruler, always cutting away from you. If you need strips that are wider than your ruler, you may use the marked lines on your cutting mat to help you measure the required width. Alternatively, use a square ruler in conjunction with your long ruler to measure the extra width.

Cutting strips

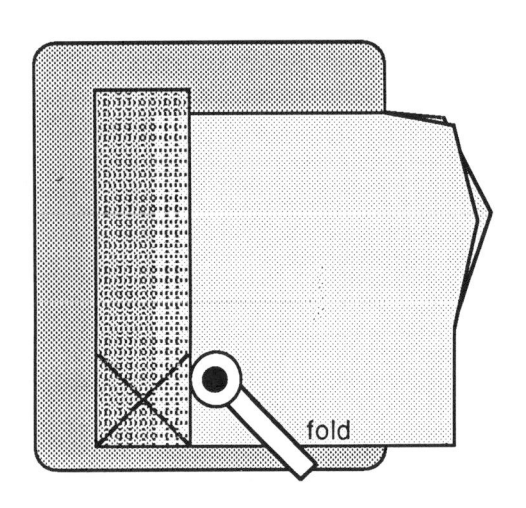

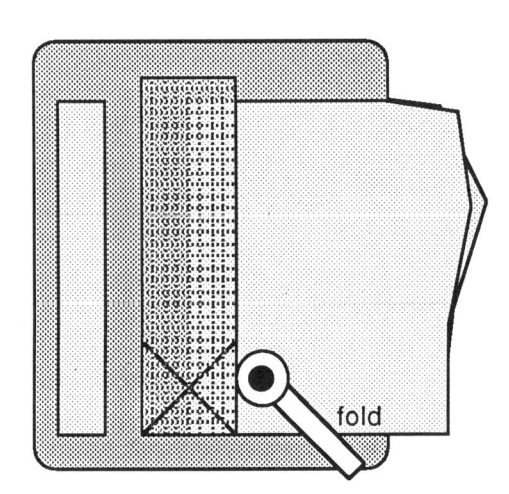

Cutting wider strips with two rulers

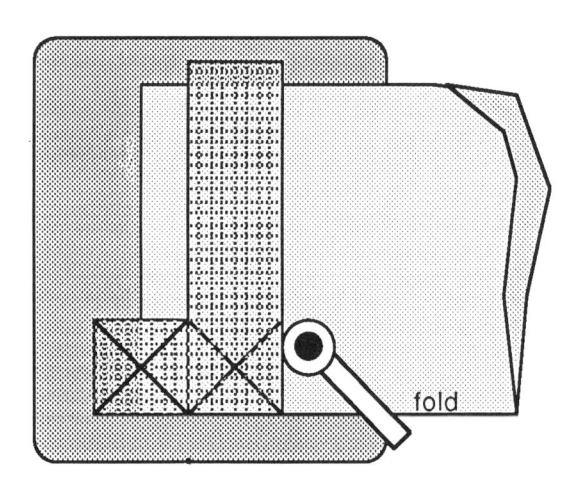

# USING YOUR ROTARY CUTTER

CUTTING BIAS-GRAIN STRIPS
1. Place your fabric on the mat in a single layer. The grain must be horizontal and vertical in front of you. You do not fold the fabric to make the first bias cut.
2. Place your ruler on the fabric, matching the diagonal 45° angle marked on the ruler to the horizontal grain. The length of your ruler should now be at a 45° angle.

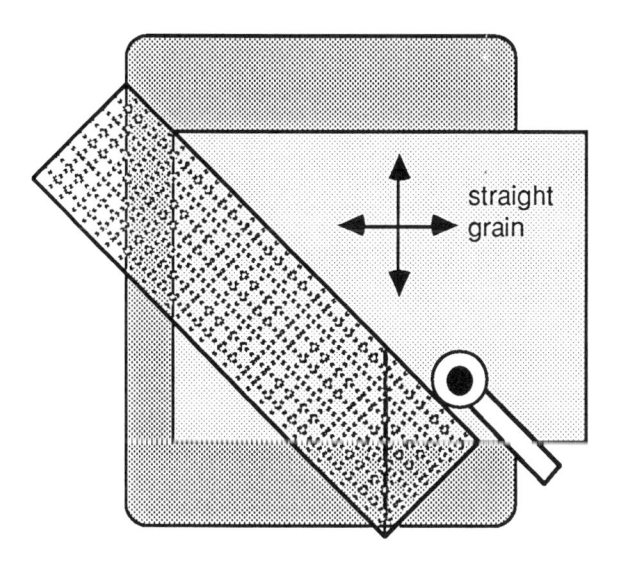

Cutting bias strips

3. Cut along the length of the ruler.

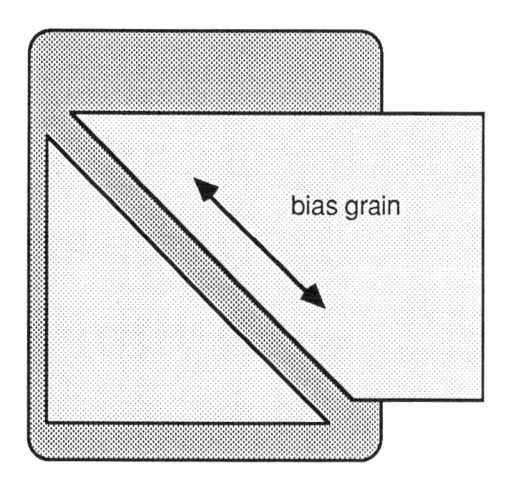

4. Turn the fabric so that the cut bias edge is now vertical in front of you. Continue cutting strips in the normal manner. You may have to fold the fabric to cut longer strips.

METRIC QUILTMAKING

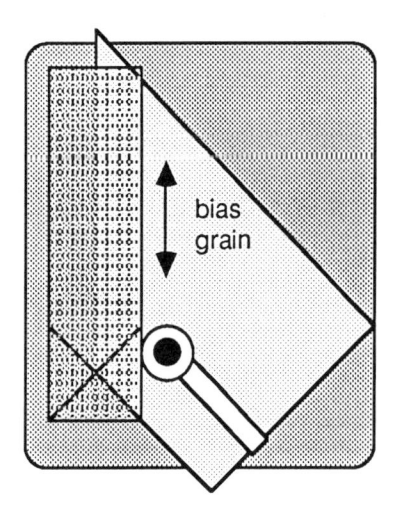

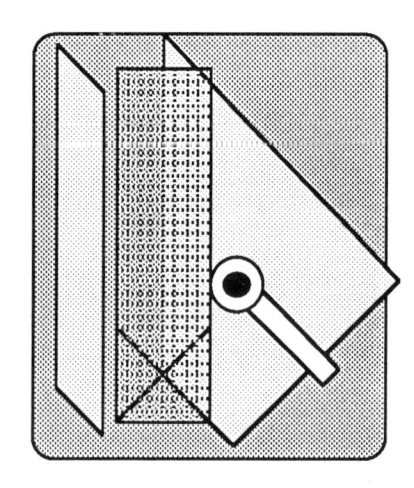

CUTTING SQUARES AND RECTANGLES
1. Determine the size required for your squares and rectangles. This will be the size of the finished patch plus 0.75 cm seam allowances all around. So, each piece must be the size of the finished patch, plus 1.5 cm.

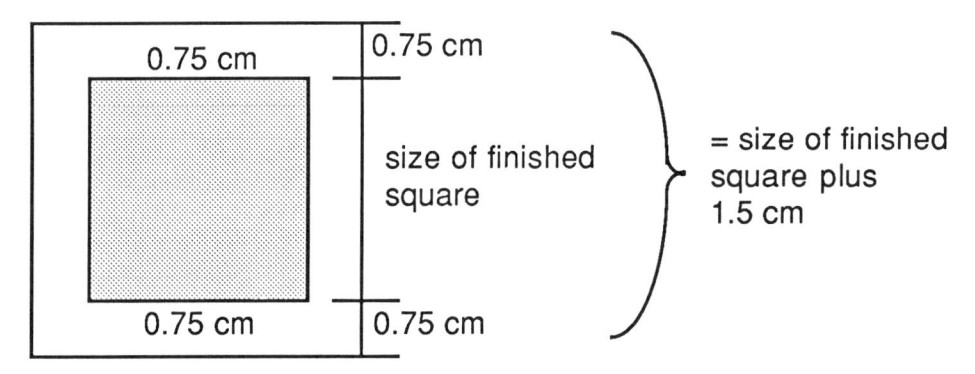

Size of squares with seams

2. Following directions for cutting strips, cut fabric into a strip the required width.
3. Square up the end of the strip (as described above for squaring up the fabric). This is done either by using two rulers, or by cutting the end square, then turning the strip around (see p. 18).
4. Place the strip horizontally in front of you, the bulk of it on the side of your dominant hand (right side for right-handers), and your squared-up edge away from your dominant hand (left side for right-handers). The small square ruler is the easiest to handle when cutting smaller pieces (the long rectangular ruler may still be used).
   When you have to cut numerous pieces, save time by marking the measurement on the ruler with masking tape. Put the tape on the top of the ruler (the printing is actually on the bottom of the ruler), so that it doesn't damage the printing.
5. Measure the size of square or rectangle required; cut.

## USING YOUR ROTARY CUTTER

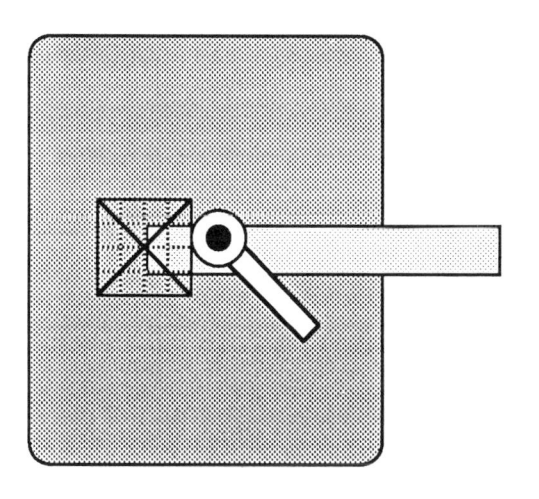

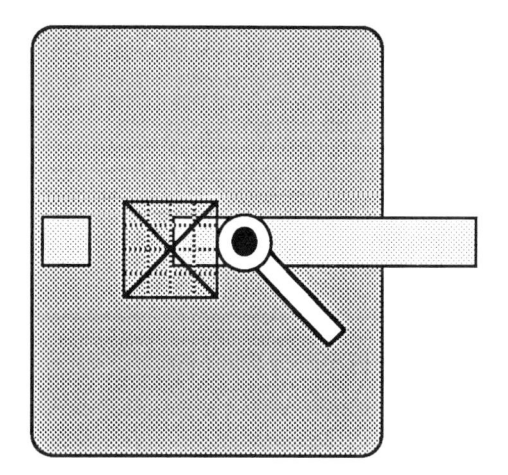

Cutting squares

CUTTING MULTIPLE SQUARES AND RECTANGLES
1. To speed cutting, cut the shapes from strips of folded fabrics, to yield two shapes from each cut.
2. If you have a cutting board marked with a grid, speed cutting even further by carefully arranging your strips exactly parallel on the horizontal lines, then cutting several of them at once with the long ruler.

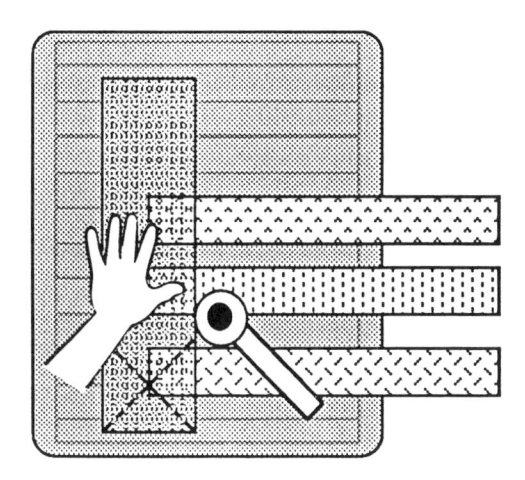

As you cut the shapes, it's very important that the strips remain exactly in place. Sometimes little threads can remain connected. When you try to move your squares in readiness to make the next cut, these threads may pull the strips out of place (they may be telling you it is time to get a new blade). To keep the strips precisely in place, the following routine is helpful:

1) Make your cut, then gently move the ruler back so that it is placed on top of the strips. Press down on the ruler to hold the strips in place.
2) While one hand keeps pressure on the ruler, use the other hand to move the already-cut squares away to the side of your mat.

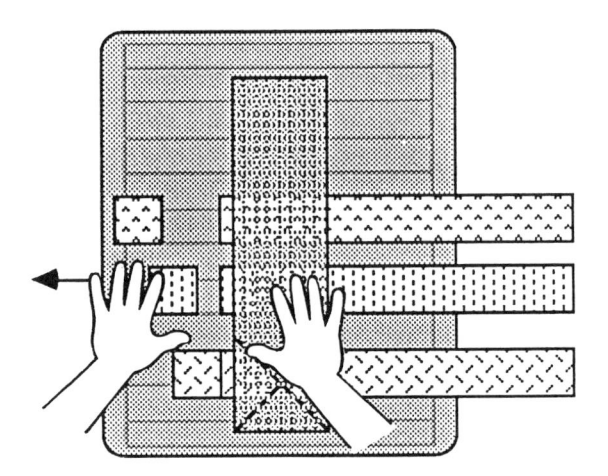

3) Gently pick up the ruler — don't disturb the strips — and place it back in the cutting position. Continue with the next cut.
4) Repeat this process along the strips. When you come near to the end, cut squares individually from the strips because it becomes too difficult to keep the small pieces precisely arranged.

CUTTING LARGE SQUARES
Large squares can be cut using the large square ruler. You may like to mark the size required with masking tape on the ruler. Place ruler on top of the fabric and cut two sides of the square. Rotate the fabric and line the already-cut edge with the ruler lines to give the size required. Cut the remaining two sides.

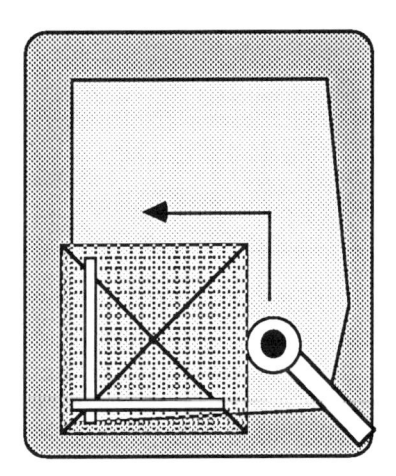

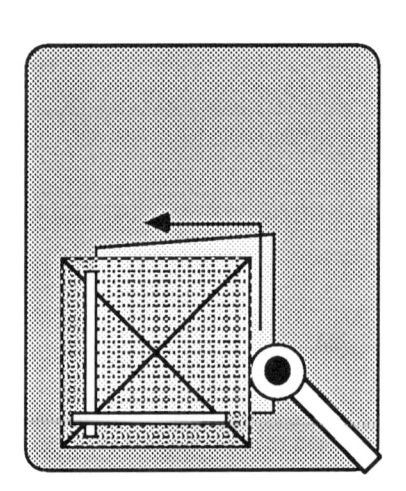

## USING YOUR ROTARY CUTTER

CUTTING HALF-SQUARE TRIANGLES
Half-square triangles are the shapes you obtain when a square is divided in half across its diagonal. This shape is the most frequently found triangle in patchwork. The half-square triangles are usually pieced in pairs to form a square. In this book, this square is called a triangle-pieced square.

The half-square triangle

There are two ways for cutting half-square triangles:
1. Cutting individual triangles
   a) Determine the size of the square you need to make the half-square triangle. It will be the size of the shorter sides of the finished triangle plus 0.75 cm seam allowances all around. This means you will cut a square the size of the shorter sides of the triangle plus 2.5 cm.

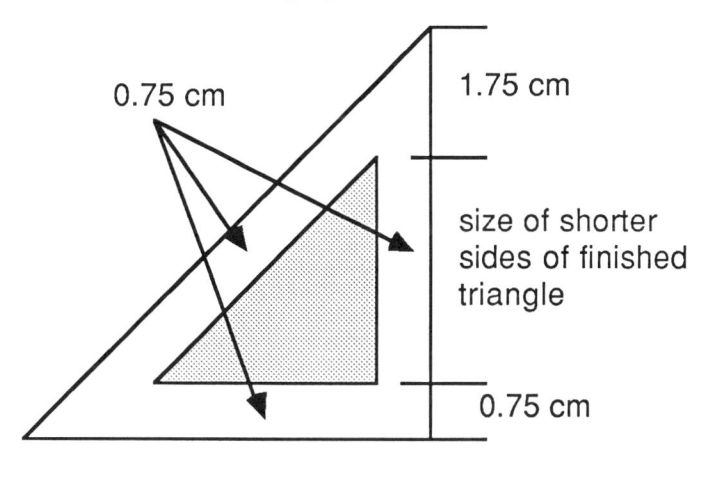

   b) Following instructions for strips and squares, cut fabric into squares the size required.
   c) Cut squares across the diagonal. Be very precise in lining up the ruler with the corners of your squares; the diagonal must be exact.
   d) Each square will yield two half-square triangles.

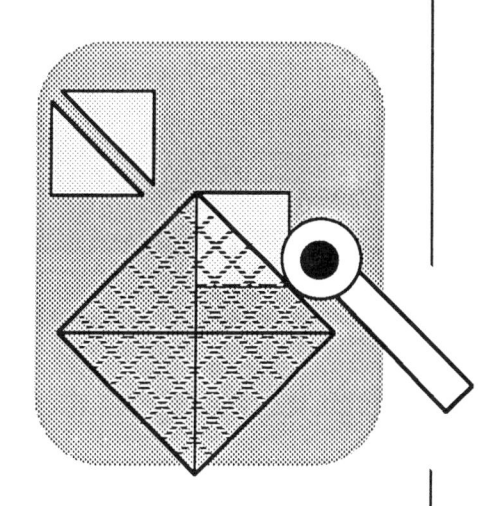

Cutting half-square triangles

# METRIC QUILTMAKING

## 2. Cutting strip-pieced triangles

Most half-square triangles in patchwork will be sewn together to make a square (in this book, this is called a triangle-pieced square). A quick and accurate method of making these triangle-pieced squares involves strip-piecing. The secret here is that **the strips are cut on the bias**. (You may, however, sometimes cut stripes and checks differently — see below.) The method is extremely accurate, because, rather than trying to sew an accurate bias seam as you do when joining two individual triangles, you cut the squares from the already-joined bias strips. The resultant squares are exactly the size you need. They have no 'ears', as can happen when you join two triangles together.

This method of making triangle-pieced squares is quick and accurate. It does, however, use a little more fabric than the process of cutting each triangle individually.

a) Following the procedure for making bias-grain strips, cut strips the same width as you require for the triangle-pieced square, including the seam allowances. If you want the triangle-pieced square to be 6.5 cm (which includes the 1.5 cm for seam allowances — the finished size of the triangle-pieced square would be 5 cm), cut the strips 6.5 cm. For 9.5 cm triangle-pieced squares (finished size 8 cm), cut the strips 9.5 cm wide, and so on.

**Cut bias strips the same width as the size of the square**

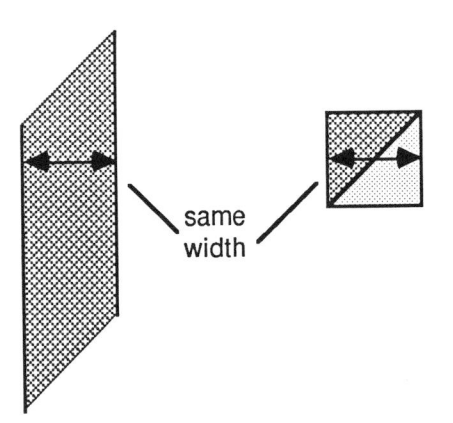

same width

With longer pieces of fabric, you may find it convenient to cut the fabric into lengths of 40—50 cm first, then to cut the bias strips.

b) Join the bias-cut strips, alternating them according to the combination of fabrics chosen. If you are only using two fabrics, then alternate strips from each. If you have many fabrics, alternate the strips according to their colour or tonal value (alternate light and dark strips, for example).

# USING YOUR ROTARY CUTTER

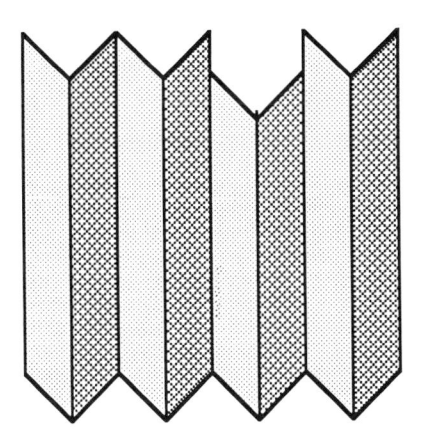

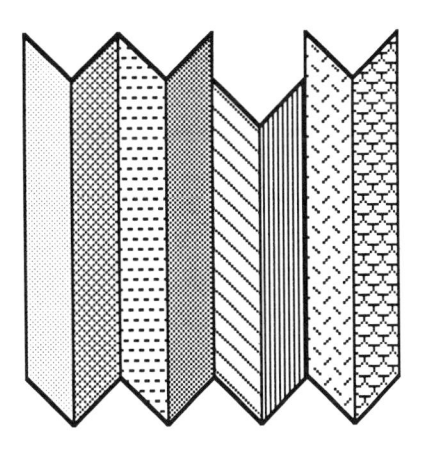

The bias strips may be joined so that one edge forms a straight line. Or, join them so that one edge forms a zigzag. Either way, begin sewing all the strips at the same end so that any unevenness in the lengths is all at the other end.

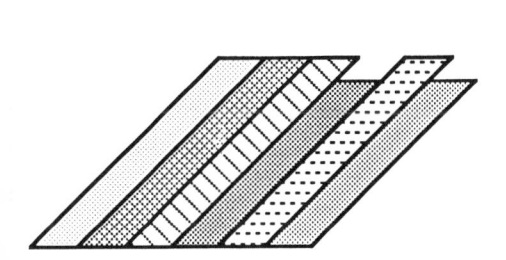

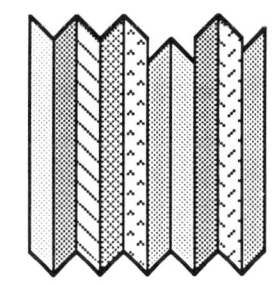

c) Press the seam allowances to the side, generally pressing either toward the darker of the fabrics or away from where any quilting lines will go.

d) Mark the size of the square you require with masking tape on your small square ruler. Place the masking tape alongside, but not on top of, the lines you will be using to measure the square.

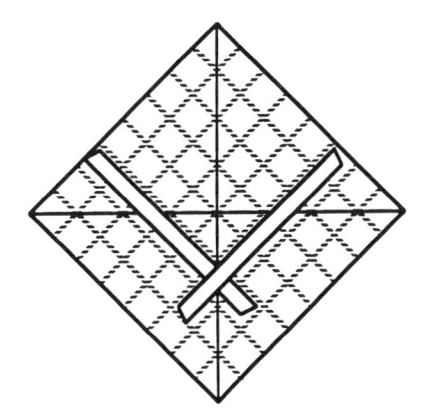

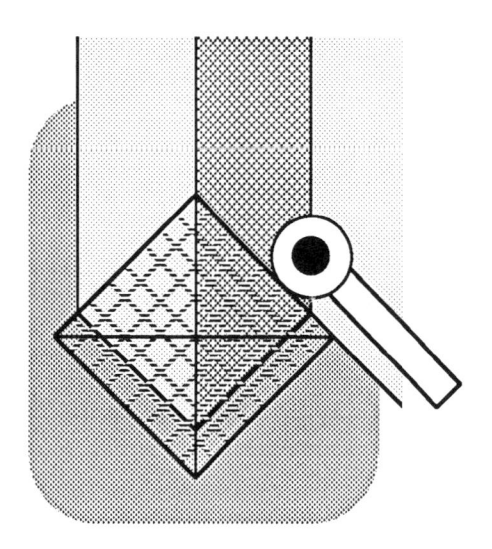

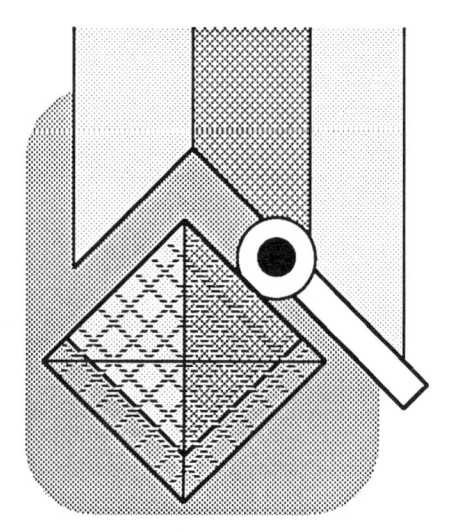

e) Place the strip-pieced fabric in front of you, its even edge at the bottom. Begin cutting squares at the bottom corner of the strip-pieced fabric, cutting always from the lowest point and working across. Note that the way you cut will vary slightly depending on the way the strips have been sewn in the first place. Using your small square ruler, match the diagonal on the ruler to the seams. Cut out two sides of the square required.

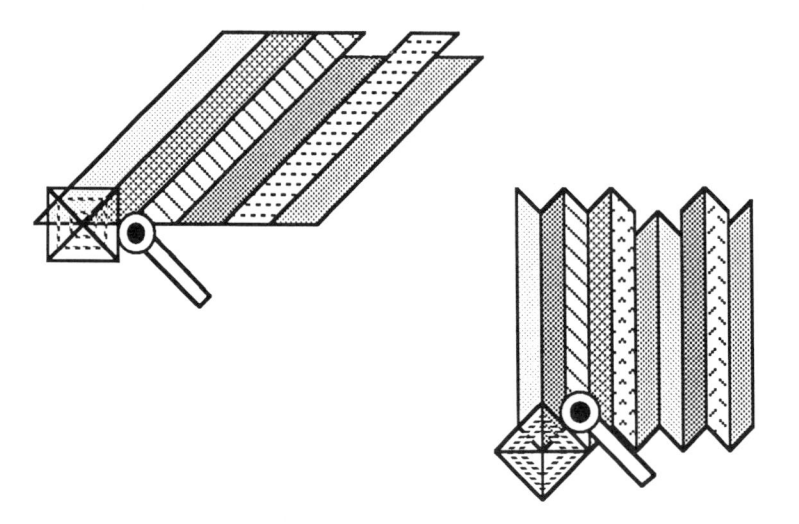

Having cut two sides, you now need to turn the pieces around and cut the remaining two sides. Generally, it is easiest to make a number of the first two cuts, stacking the resulting pieces into a pile as you go. Turn the pile around and recut the remaining two sides of each square.

## USING YOUR ROTARY CUTTER

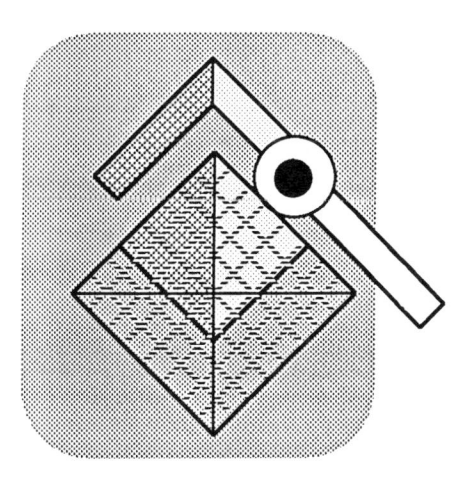

f) Save the off-cuts which remain from the sides of the outer strips after the squares have been cut. These can be recut to make individual triangles.

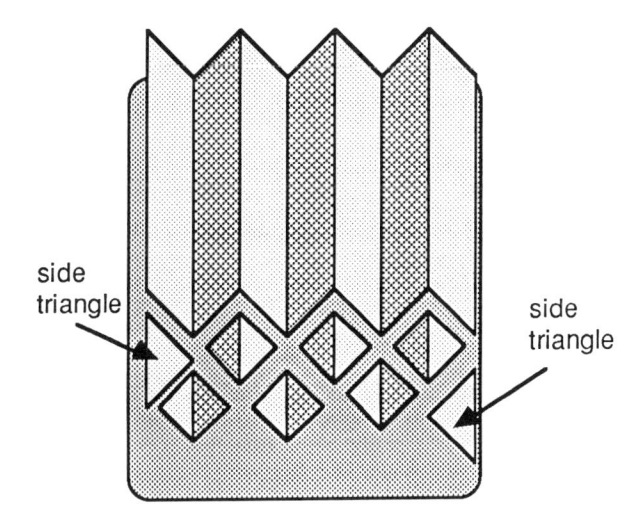

### CHECKS AND STRIPES

When you use checks and stripes in triangle-pieced squares, you may want the lines in the pattern to go in a particular direction in the finished patchwork. In this situation, you may need to cut the strips on the straight grain, rather than the bias. Be aware that squares made from these strips will have some bias edges. These edges will be inclined to stretch and will need careful sewing.

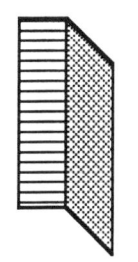

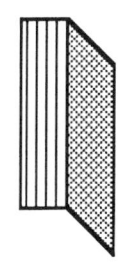

## CUTTING QUARTER-SQUARE TRIANGLES

Quarter-square triangles are the shapes you obtain when a square is divided into quarters across its two diagonals.

**The quarter-square triangle**

1. Determine the size of the square you need in order to make the quarter-square triangle. This size will be the length of the longest side of the finished triangle, plus 0.75 cm seam allowances all around. You will be cutting a square the size of the longest side of the finished triangle plus 3.5 cm.

**Size of quarter-square triangle with seams**

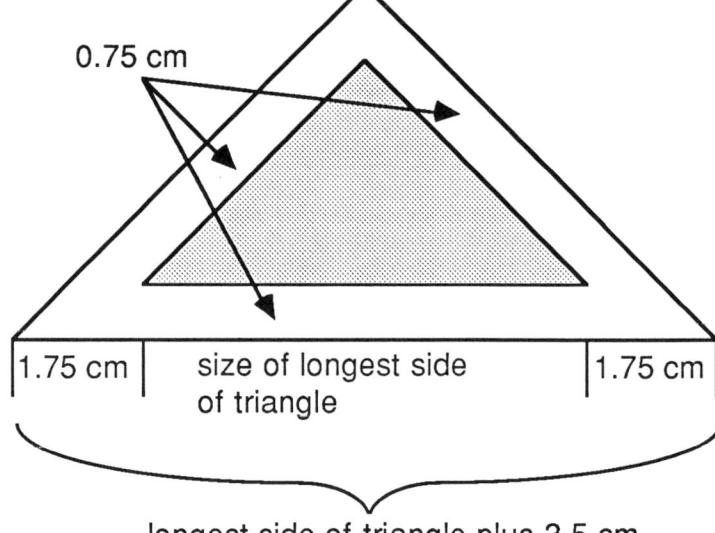

0.75 cm

1.75 cm | size of longest side of triangle | 1.75 cm

= longest side of triangle plus 3.5 cm

2. Cut fabric into strips, then recut the strips into squares the size required.
3. Cut squares across one diagonal. Without moving the pieces in any way so that the cut square remains exactly in place, recut the square across the other diagonal.
4. Each square will yield four quarter-square triangles.

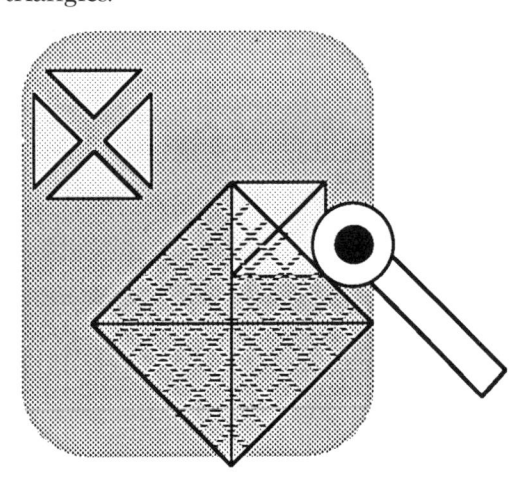

**Cutting quarter square triangles**

# SEWING

### THE 0.75 CM SEAM ALLOWANCE

The foundation of successful metric patchwork is the 0.75 cm seam allowance. This is the width added to all pieces as you cut them out, so this **must** be the width of the seam allowance you sew in order to make all the pieces fit accurately together.

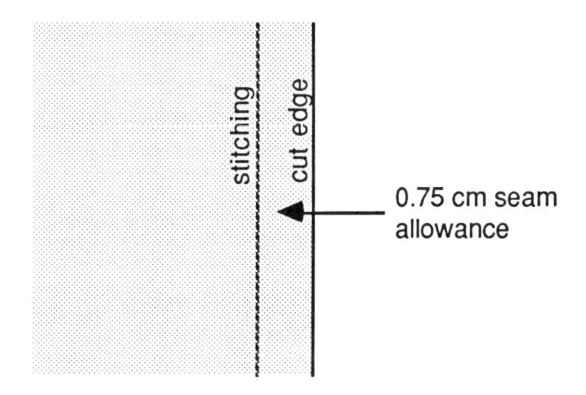

← 0.75 cm seam allowance

We are calling the seam allowance 0.75 cm because quilters usually use centimetre measurements. But in the metric system, the same measure may also be called 7.5 mm.

The 0.75 cm allowance was chosen because it allows for sensibly sized multiples: every patch you cut out must have 0.75 cm added to every side, making the total either 1.5 cm (for squares, rectangles and strips), 2.5 cm (for squares which are cut to make half-square triangles) or 3.5 cm (for squares which are cut to make quarter-square triangles).

A 0.5 cm width would be too narrow to sew comfortably, while a 1 cm seam would be too bulky and would get in the way of hand quilting.

SETTING UP THE MACHINE FOR A 0.75 cm
SEAM ALLOWANCE
1. Measure the width of your sewing machine foot. The width you are measuring is the distance between the needle and the right-hand edge of the foot (as you are facing, looking at it). Many machines have feet which give this 0.75 cm width exactly . If this is your situation, life is easy as you need do nothing more than match the cut edges of your pieces with the edge of your sewing machine foot.

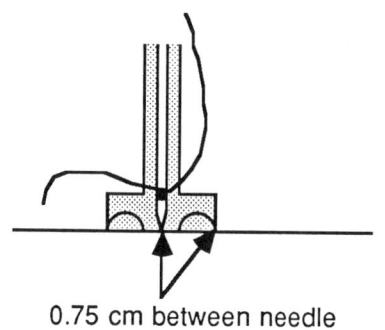

0.75 cm between needle and edge of the foot

# METRIC QUILTMAKING

0.5 cm (5 mm) graph paper

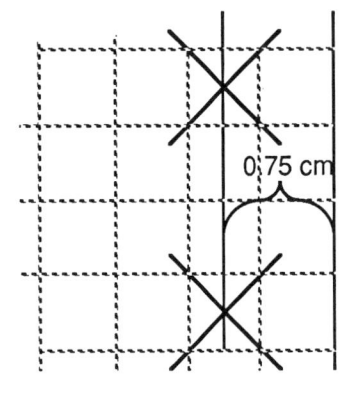

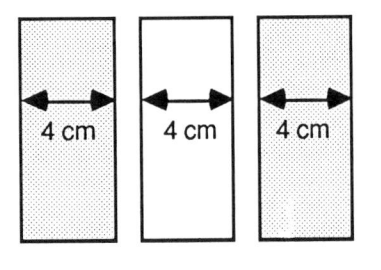

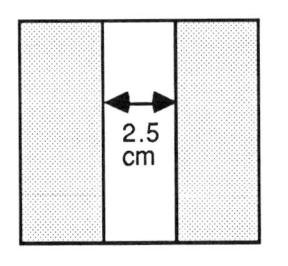

2. If your machine has a foot which is either wider or narrower than 0.75 cm, there are two possibilities for making the correct seam allowance.

a) Mark the seam allowance on the plate of the machine below the machine foot. Find the 0.75 cm width and mark this distance with a line on your presser-foot plate. A piece of masking tape is useful for marking the distance. Or you could draw a line with permanent-ink pen.

One way of finding the correct distance is to use a small piece of metric graph paper. Draw two lines on it which are exactly 0.75 cm apart. Cut down the edge of one of the lines. If you can only find graph paper marked in 0.5 cm squares, locate the centre of a square exactly by drawing diagonal lines across it to give the 0.25 cm measurement. Do this twice; join the two centres. Now measure the 0.75 cm distance from this line. Cut precisely along the edge of this line.

Place the piece of graph paper under your machine foot and centre the needle on the line you have drawn. The edge you have cut then gives you the exact 0.75 cm width.

Another possibility is to use a ruler with the 0.75 cm seam allowance marked. Place the ruler under the foot of the machine, lining up the needle with the line marking the 0.75 cm line. You can then draw or place the masking tape along the edge of the ruler. Do this very carefully — you do **not** want the needle to come down on the ruler.

b) Move the needle to the right or left to position it the correct distance from the edge of the machine foot. Consult your sewing machine guide about how to move the needle into a different position; machines vary in how this is done. Use the small piece of graph paper with the 0.75 cm seam allowance marked (see above) to find the correct needle position. Place the graph paper under your machine foot, the cut edge exactly matching the edge of the foot. Move the needle so it will come down exactly on the marked 0.75 cm line. Keep the small piece of graph paper next to your machine to use every time you need to set the needle.

3. Checking for accuracy

Whatever arrangements you make to sew the 0.75 cm seam allowance, it is the finished and accurate result which is all important. Check your accuracy by cutting three strips of fabric, each 4 cm wide. Sew the strips together, press the seams to one side, and measure the finished size of the centre strip. It should be exactly 2.5 cm wide. If it is not this width, alter the way you make the seam allowance until it is exact.

## SEWING

### SETTING UP YOUR SEWING SPACE
Set up your sewing machine with space at your left for the laid-out quilt block. Have the iron handy for pressing. Keep thread snippers just by your machine. A plastic bag taped to the edge of the table is useful for neatly collecting all the thread.

### GENERAL TECHNIQUE FOR SEWING THE SEAMS
1. Place the cut-out pieces right sides together, matching the edges precisely.
2. Place the patchwork under the machine, precisely lining up the work so that you make the 0.75 cm seam allowances. This may be done by either by matching the cut edges of the patchwork to the edge of the presser foot, or by lining up the patchwork with a line marked with either pen or masking tape (as described above).
3. Keeping the exact 0.75 cm seam throughout, begin sewing from one cut edge and sew down the seam to the opposite cut edge. There is no need to backtrack. Snip off ends immediately after sewing each seam.

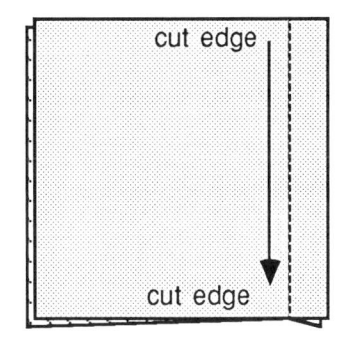

### CHAIN PIECING
In 'chain piecing', a series of seams is sewn together in one operation. Don't stop to cut off the threads after each seam. All the pieces are then connected by short threads.

Chain piecing can speed up sewing because it minimises starting and stopping. When the 'chain' is finished, the parts can be snipped apart and the beginning and ending threads cut off.

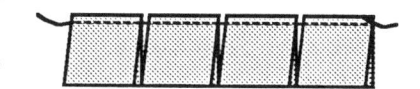

### PINNING
A minimum of pinning is required if you cut and sew a precise seam allowance. To increase accuracy, pin at seam junctions so that these meet neatly. Place a pin either side of the seam junction, pinning at right angles to the seam line.

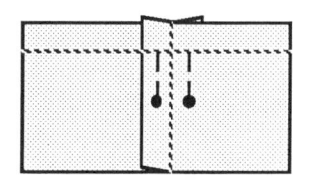

## PRESSING

Press the seams together to one side after sewing. All seams must be pressed before going on to any cross seams. This doesn't mean that each seam needs to be pressed immediately after sewing — you may choose to sew the seams of a couple of pieces, then press them all before going on to the next bit of the block. Whatever method you choose, never sew across an unpressed seam; inaccuracy will be the result.

Press on the right side of your patchwork. The seams must be pressed away from the point of the iron.

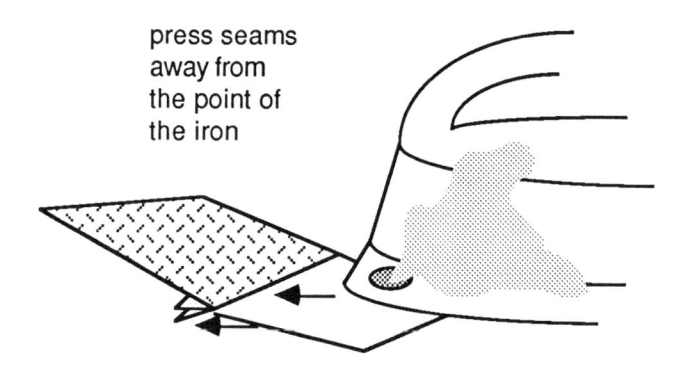

*press seams away from the point of the iron*

Press the seams to whichever side suits the particular seam you are sewing. There are many factors to consider to determine what is appropriate for your particular seam:

1) Press the seams so that they lie in alternate directions at the seam junctions. This method helps ensure the seams meet accurately at junctions; it also distributes the bulk to make the seams lie flatter.

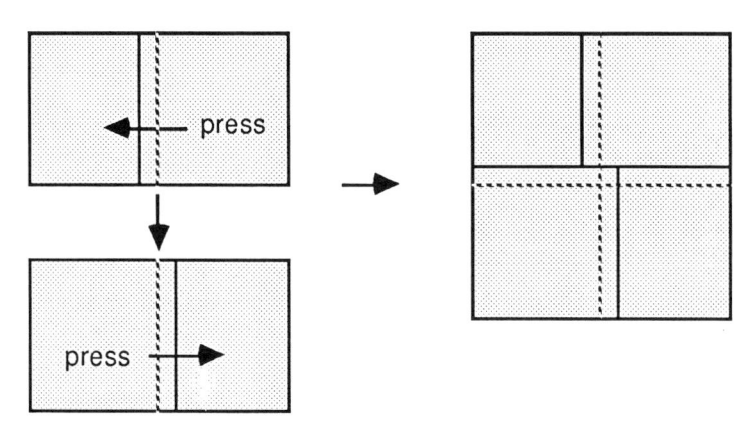

It is not possible to sew all seam junctions this way. Because of previously pressed and sewn seams, you will sometimes find you have no alternative but to have junctions which do not have seams pressed in opposite directions.

2) Press the seams toward the darker fabric to avoid having a shadow showing through. This

may be a consideration if you are sewing a particularly light fabric.

3) Press the seams away from where any quilting will go; it is much easier to quilt along the side of the seam where there are no seam allowances.

4) Press the seams so that they will lie flat. Do not create unnecessary bulk. Some seam allowances seem to have a mind of their own. In these instances, it may be better to give in to the direction they want to go.

### BLOCK CONSTRUCTION

Quilts are usually constructed in blocks. Blocks are the units of patchwork that go to make up a quilt top.

1. Lay out the cut-out block. This is essential, no matter whether you are sewing a simple block or a complicated one. If the block is not laid out correctly, it is all too easy to sew pieces together so that one (or more) of them is turned around and the block pattern goes askew. Follow the correct procedure and you won't make time-consuming errors.

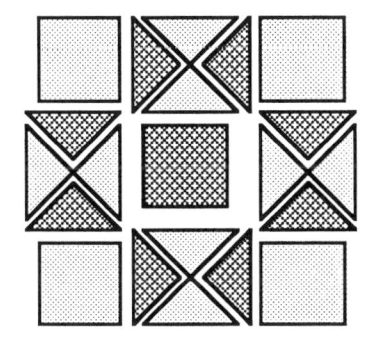

2. Sew the smaller pieces together first, so that the block becomes a set of squares.

Half-square triangles are joined by sewing across the diagonal seam. When the seam is finished and pressed, little corner 'ears' will stick out at the end of the seam. Trim these 'ears' away.

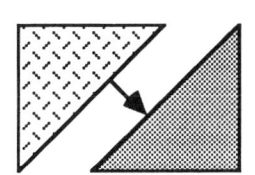

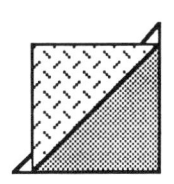

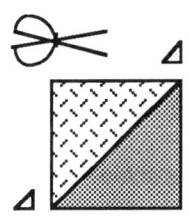

Note that with the strip-pieced method of making triangle-pieced squares, this job has already been done for you.

Quarter-square triangles, are joined in three steps:
a) join two adjacent triangles together;
b) join the remaining two triangles together;
c) join the already-sewn triangles together to make a square, matching the seams carefully at the centre. (The seams in the two lots of triangles should always be pressed in opposite directions to make this seam easy to match.) Trim off the 'ears'.

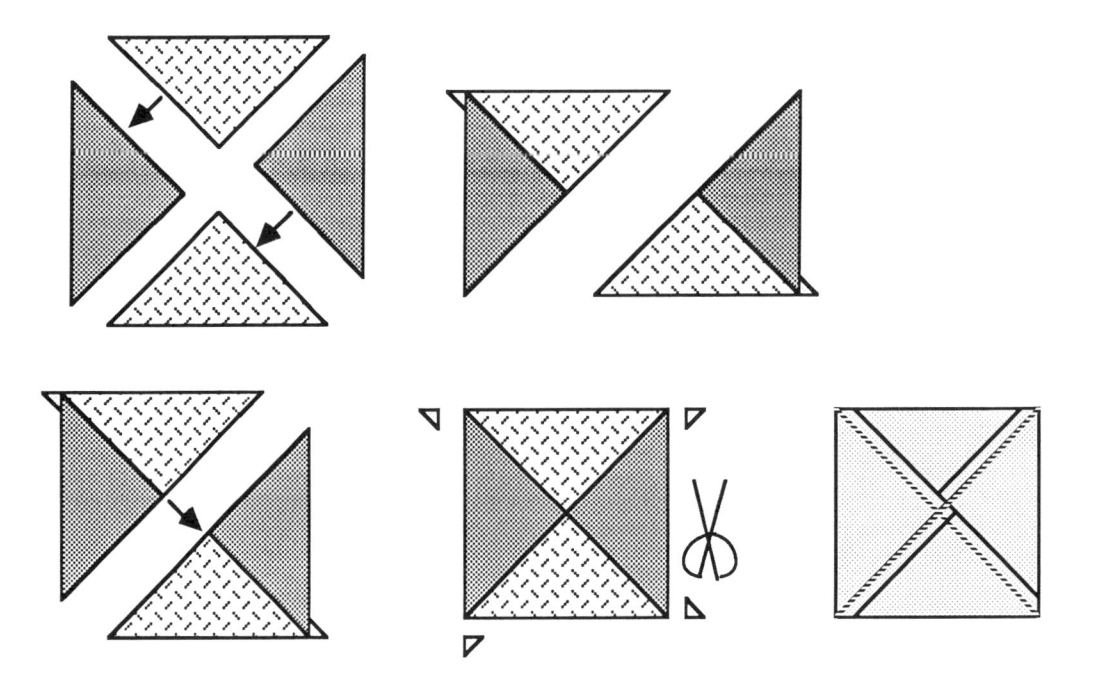

Small squares can be joined to make rectangles which then must be joined to make larger squares. Sometimes these smaller squares may consist of already-pieced units such as triangle-pieced squares.

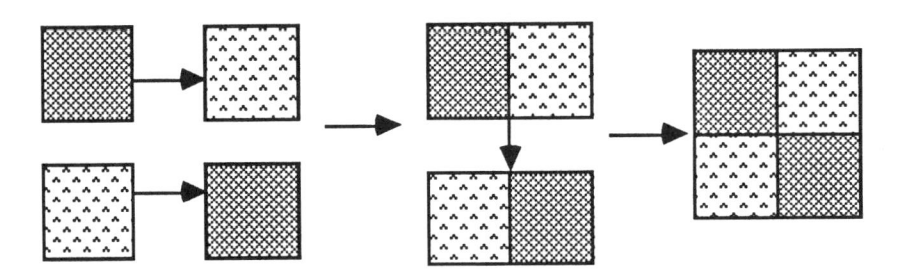

3. Sew the squares into rows, then sew the rows together to make the block.

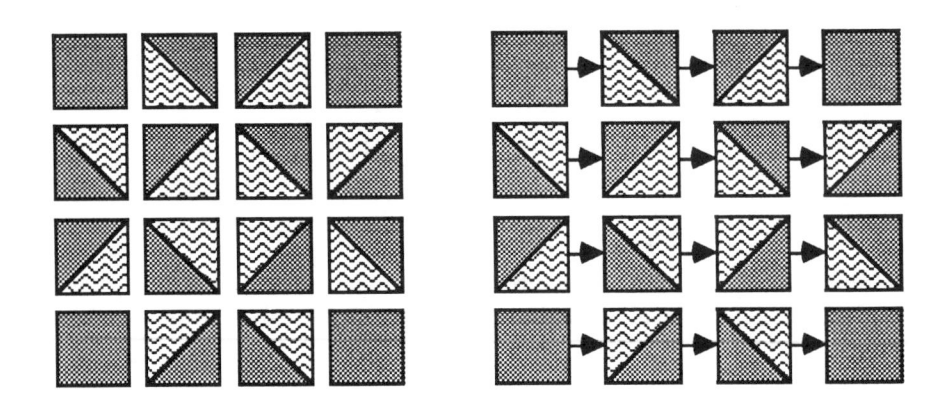

# SEWING

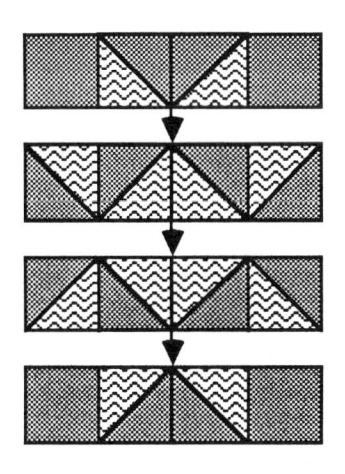

When you have sewn the squares into rows, press the seams of alternate rows in opposite directions. This way, the seam junctions will be neat and accurate.

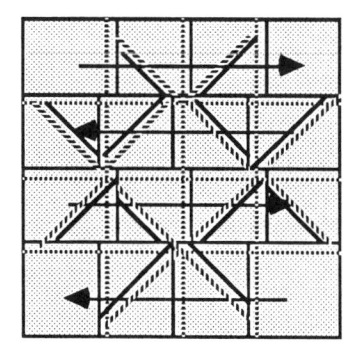

CHAIN PIECING A BLOCK
Here is another block construction method which is particularly useful for sewing blocks which are made entirely of squares. It can also be used when the block is at the stage when any smaller pieces have been already joined to make squares.

1. Lay out the block, each piece in its correct position. We have numbered each square in the block in the diagram, so that you can see easily which pieces go where.

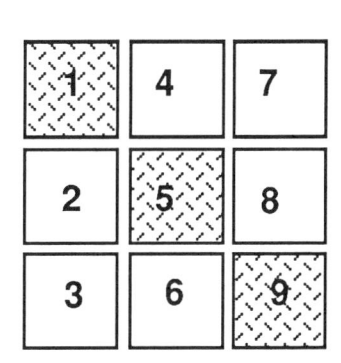

# METRIC QUILTMAKING

2. Stack the squares vertically into piles. Begin with the square in the bottom left-hand corner, put the next one on top, and continue until you get to the top of the vertical row. Then stack the next vertical row, and so on. Ultimately, you will have a row of little stacks as shown below.

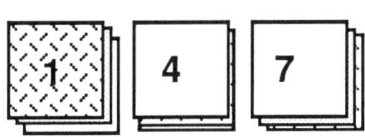

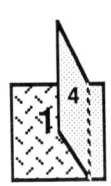

3. Pick up two patches from the top of the two left-hand stacks. Keeping them correctly oriented, place the two patches right sides together and sew a seam down the right-hand side of the pieces. Stop your machine at the cut edge of the very end of the seam, leaving the patches under the presser foot.

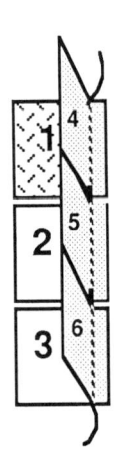

4. Pick up the next two patches from the same two left-hand stacks. Again, put them right sides together. Place them under the presser foot, butting them right up to the previous two patches. Sew down the seam, again stopping at the cut edge at the end of the seam. This is called chain piecing because you keep on sewing without cutting the threads between each seam.

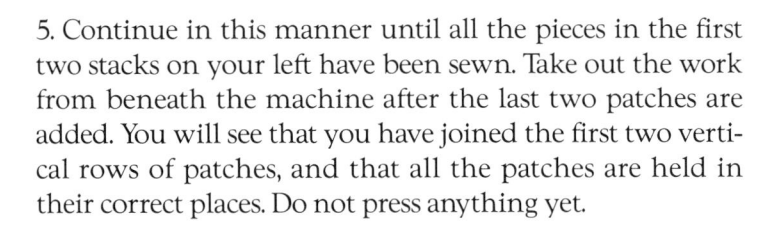

5. Continue in this manner until all the pieces in the first two stacks on your left have been sewn. Take out the work from beneath the machine after the last two patches are added. You will see that you have joined the first two vertical rows of patches, and that all the patches are held in their correct places. Do not press anything yet.

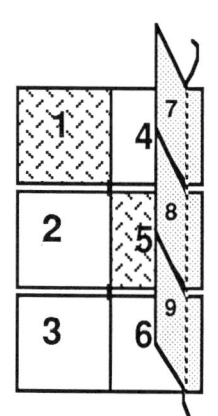

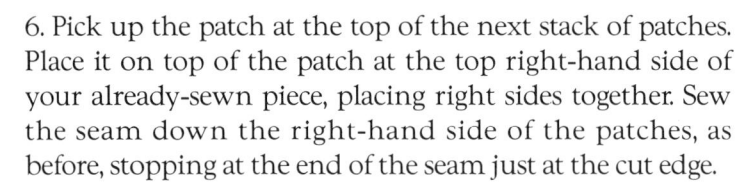

6. Pick up the patch at the top of the next stack of patches. Place it on top of the patch at the top right-hand side of your already-sewn piece, placing right sides together. Sew the seam down the right-hand side of the patches, as before, stopping at the end of the seam just at the cut edge.

7. Pick up the next patch in the stack. Place it under the presser foot and sew down the next seam, stopping as before.

8. Continue in this manner until the stack is finished. Pull the work out from under the machine.

9. Sew patches in any remaining stack (or stacks) in place.

40

# SEWING

When all the patches from all the stacks are sewn, you will see that the block is joined completely in horizontal rows, with short threads holding the rows in place.

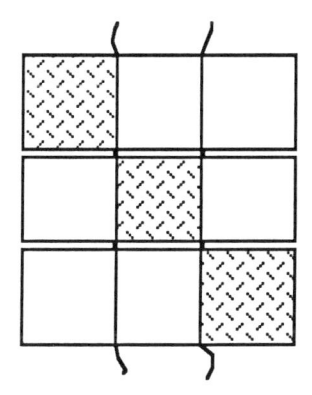

Your block is neatly arranged with every patch in its correct place. It is now ready for pressing. Press the seams in alternate rows in opposite directions.

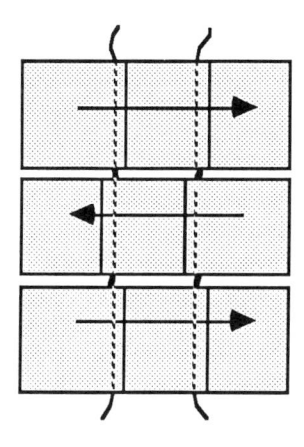

10. Sew the rows together to complete the block. There is no need to snip the little loops which join the rows. Press the block after all the seams are finished.

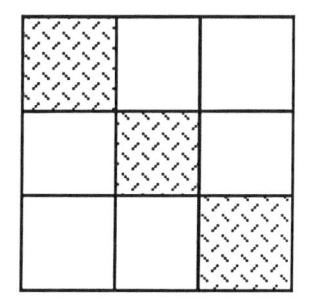

## Appliqué

A few of the blocks illustrated in this book include some appliqué strips in an otherwise pieced block, such as the Basket block (see p. 85).

Strips are cut on the bias grain (see p. 23) so that they will curve. The cut width of the strips will be double the finished size of the strip, plus 1.5 cm for seam allowances. For example, for a 1 cm-wide strip, cut a bias strip 3.5 cm wide. Fold the strip in half lengthwise, wrong sides together. Stitch a 0.75 cm seam down the cut edge. Trim the seam allowance to 0.3 cm (3 mm). Press the strip flat so that the seam and seam allowance are at the back of the strip. Pin and tack (baste) the strip in place, then hand sew down each side. Note that the strips are sewn to the appropriate piece in the block before the piece is sewn into the block; this way, the ends will be neatly hidden in the seam.

# QUILT CONSTRUCTION

## BLOCK WORK

### LAYING OUT THE BLOCKS

Once the blocks are complete, you may need to lay them out to determine their correct position in the quilt. This is particularly important if you are making a scrap quilt where colours and tonal values need careful placement. Use your flannelette sheet, or pin the blocks onto a large pin-board. Balance the colours and tonal values as you pin, moving the blocks around as required. Stand back repeatedly to check the overall effect — this is where a door peep-hole, camera, binoculars used in reverse, or reducing glass is invaluable.

### ASSEMBLING THE BLOCKS

There are two ways to join the blocks. The main way is to join them in rows and then to join the rows together. However, for some quilts, the chain-sewing method is very effective.

1. Joining the blocks

Blocks are generally joined by sewing them into rows, then sewing these rows together to make the quilt top.

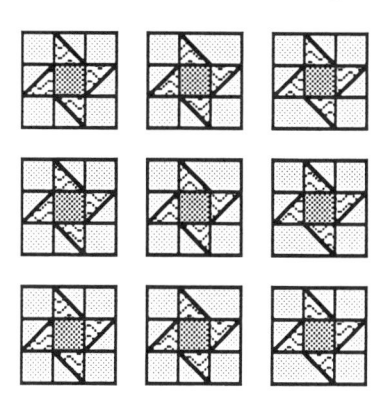

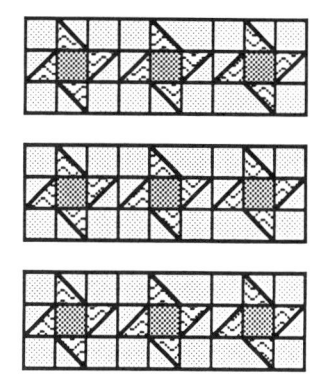

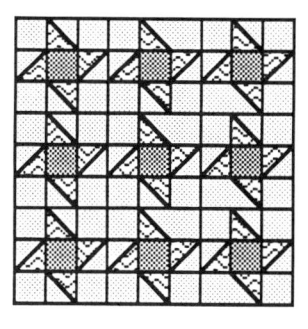

If sashing is to be added, sashing strips are included between the blocks when these are joined into rows. When the rows are being joined, sashing strips are added between the rows.

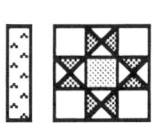

# METRIC QUILTMAKING

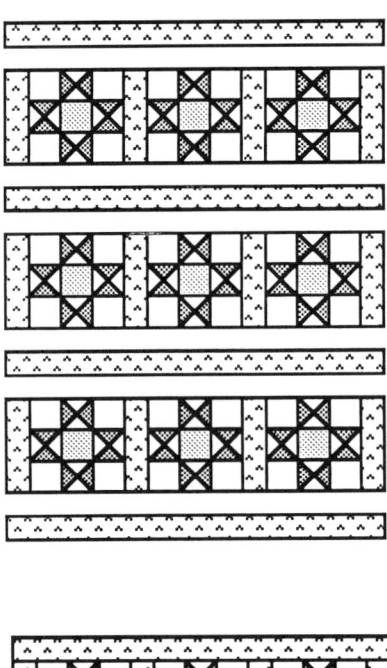

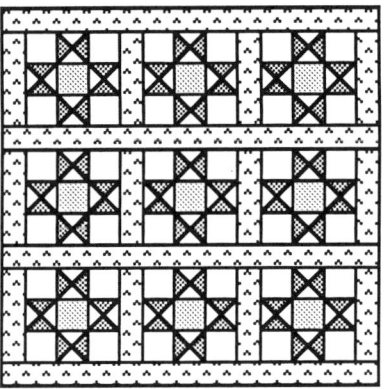

When sewing sashing strips between rows, sew the strips to one row of blocks, then measure and mark with pins (pin mark) the other side of the strip to show where the blocks of the next rows should line up. Match these pin-marks to the edge of the blocks when you are sewing the next row.

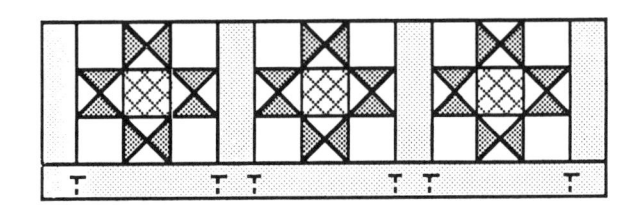

Sometimes sashing strips are pieced with squares in the corners between the blocks; these squares are called 'posts'.

# QUILT CONSTRUCTION

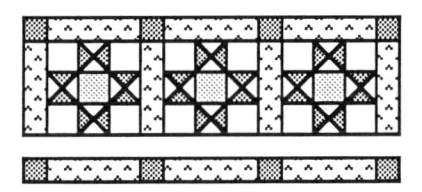

Diagonal blocks are also sewn together into rows. Begin in one corner and work in diagonal rows across to the opposite corner. The edges and corners will be filled with either quarter-squares and half-squares which are sewn into their appropriate rows.

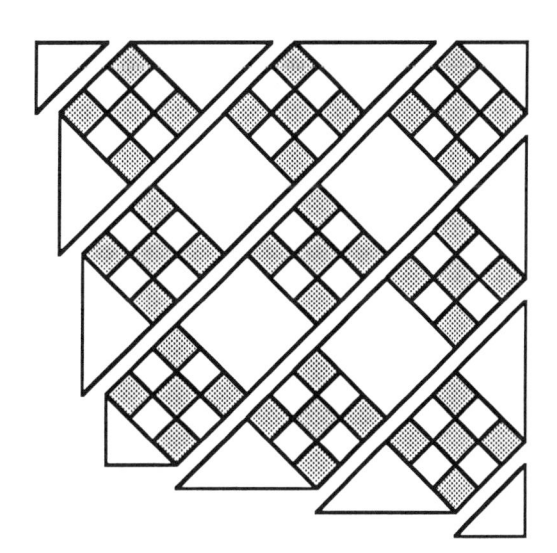

## 2. The chain-sewing quilt construction method

This method employs the same procedure described for chain-sewing block construction (see p. 39), only this time you are putting blocks together instead of the squares in a block. Use this method when there is no sashing between blocks.

1) Lay out the blocks in their final positions. Place a pin as a marker in the top left-hand corner of the top left-hand block.

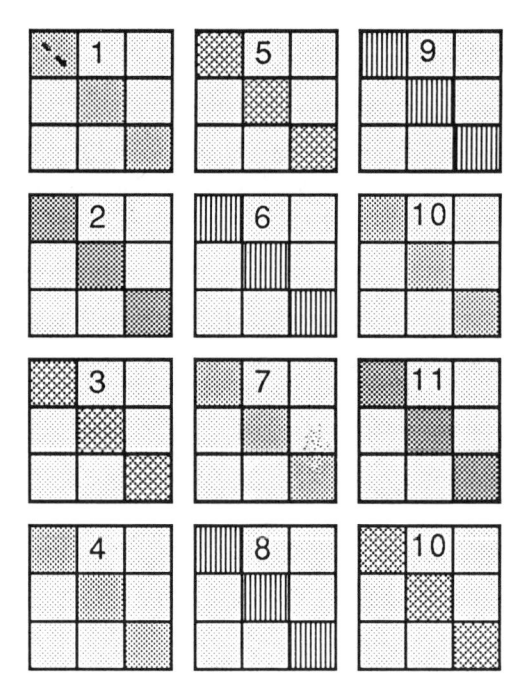

2) Starting at the bottom left, stack the first vertical row of blocks into a pile. The block you marked with a pin should now be on top of the pile, right side upwards.

3) Stack the blocks in the second vertical row of blocks, again beginning from the bottom. Leave the remaining blocks pinned up in their place — it is better to stack up the piles just before sewing them to avoid confusion and losing your place.

4) Take the two blocks from the top of the stacks. Place them right sides together and sew a seam down the right-hand side. Stop sewing just at the end of the seam at the bottom edge of the blocks, but do not remove the blocks from the machine.

5) Pick up the next two blocks. Place them right sides together, put them under the machine next to the previously sewn blocks, and again sew the seam down the right-hand side. Stop at the edge of the blocks as before.

6) Continue in this manner until all the blocks in the two stacks have been sewn. Do not snip the threads. Do not press yet.

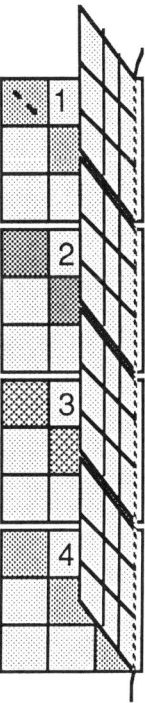

7) Go back to your laid-out quilt and stack up the next vertical row of blocks, beginning from the bottom.

8) Your already-sewn piece should have the pin marking its top left corner so that you do not inadvertently sew the next row in the wrong place. Sew the blocks from your third stack to the already-sewn first two rows, using the same method as before. Do not press yet.

9) Continue in this manner until all the blocks have been joined. Your quilt should have every block in its correct place, with the horizontal rows of blocks connected

to each other by threads. Now it is time to press. Press the seams in each alternate row in the opposite direction, so that the seam junctions lay flat. Press from the right side. You may find it easier to press alternate seams from different sides of your ironing board.

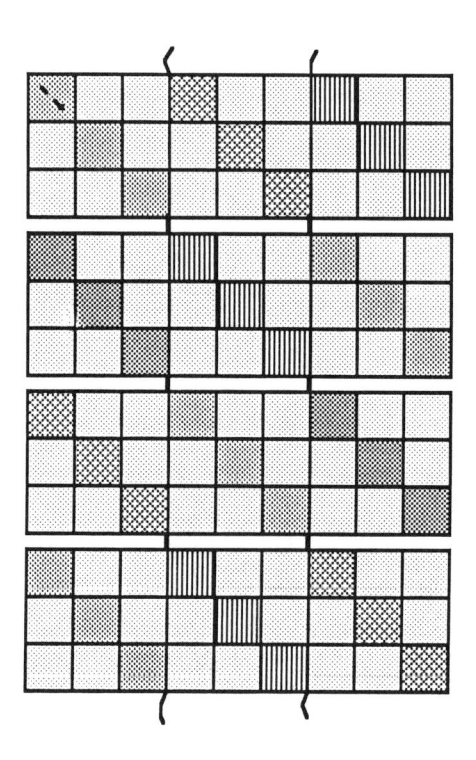

10) Sew the horizontal seams and press the quilt top.

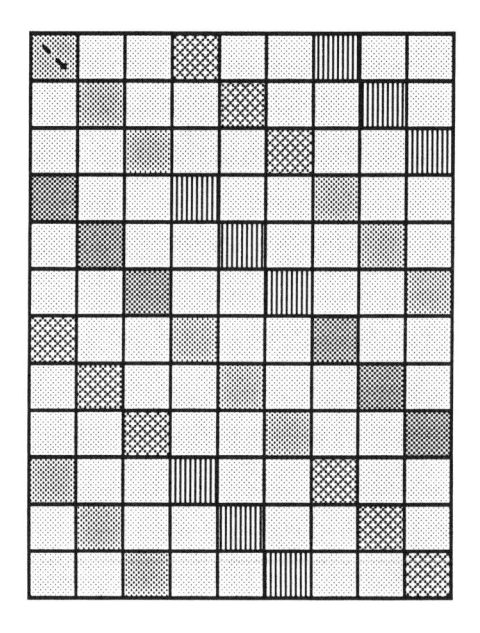

# QUILT CONSTRUCTION

### ADDING BORDERS

THE IMPORTANCE OF MEASURING

Measuring correctly is the most important procedure to observe when adding borders, and the one thing that is most frequently ignored in quilt construction. **You must always measure a quilt through its centre to find the correct length for the borders.** Wavy and wonky borders are the result of measuring a quilt along its sides instead of through its centre. The sides of a quilt top often may have stretched, giving you a false measurement. By using a centre measurement, you can correct any stretching or distortion which has occurred at the sides of the quilt. You will also ensure your quilt has the same measurement on both sides.

ADDING THE BORDER STRIPS

You can add border strips with squared corners or with mitred ones.

1. Squared corners

a) Lay out the pressed quilt top on a flat surface and measure it vertically through the centre. Cut two side strips this length. Place a pin at the centre of the two border strips and at the centre of each side of the quilt. This is called pin-marking in halves, and on a large quilt, you may need to pin-mark both the quilt and borders in quarters. Matching the marking pins, pin and stitch the side borders in place. Press the seams.

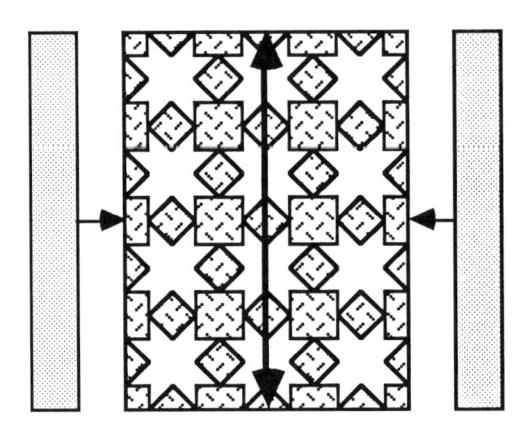

b) Lay out quilt again. Measure the quilt top across the centre horizontally (you will now be measuring the already-added borders, as well as the centre of the quilt). Cut the border strips the required length. Pin-mark the centre of the strips and the quilt top, then pin and sew the borders in place, matching the marking pins.

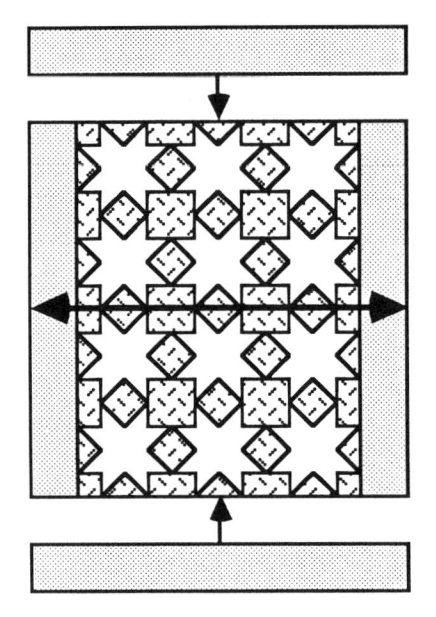

# QUILT CONSTRUCTION

2. Mitred corners

a) Lay out the pressed quilt top on a flat surface, and measure the quilt through the centre. Cut border strips this length, plus the width of the borders at each end, plus a little extra to have as leeway. Pin-mark the centre of all four strips. Pin-mark the centre of the sides of the quilt top.

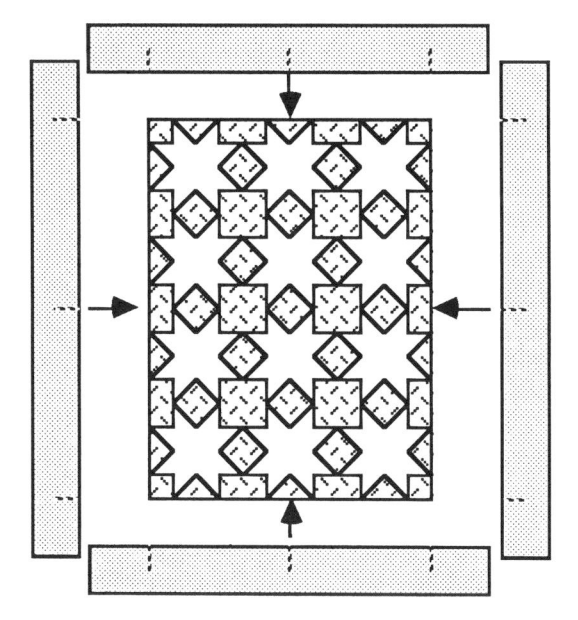

b) Lay a border strip across the centre of the quilt, matching the centre pin-mark of the border strip to the centre of the quilt. Pin-mark the border strip at the side edges. Pin and stitch the border to the sides of the quilt; be careful on the corners to stitch exactly to the corner where the seams would meet, then backtrack — do **not** sew into the seam allowances at the corners.

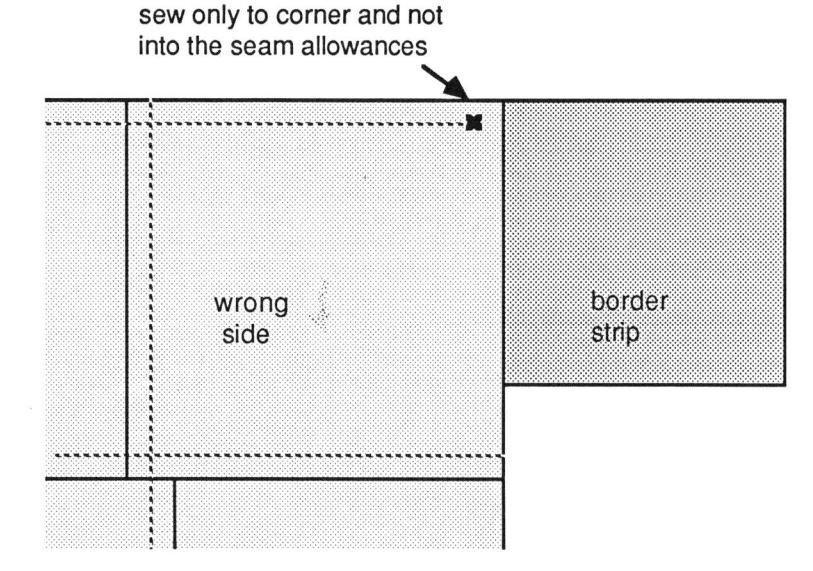

c) Repeat the same process for the remaining three sides, again being careful not to sew into the corner seam allowances.

d) Working on each corner in turn, fold the quilt so that the border strips are horizontally aligned, with the right sides together, and making a diagonal fold out from the corner where the strips meet. Pin the border strips to each other. Using the diagonal line on the square ruler, mark a 45° angle out towards the corner, drawing the line exactly from the point where your stitching stopped at the corner. Stitch along this line, again stitching precisely from the corner.

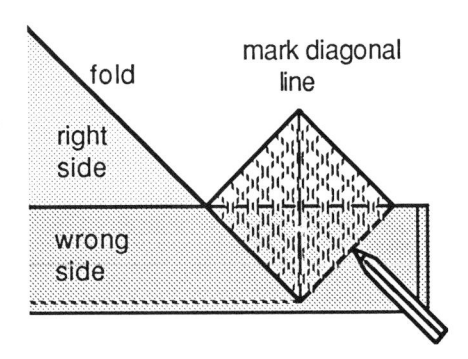

e) Trim the excess fabric. Press this seam open.

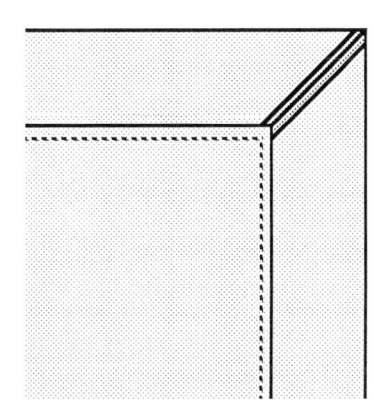

## QUILTING

Quilting is the stitching which joins the three layers of the quilt — the top, the batting and the backing. It may be done by hand or machine.

The important thing to remember about quilting is that it is not the stitching which forms the pattern. Rather, it is the highlights and shadows formed by the quilting that create the design. This happens because the quilting compresses the stitched areas so that they form little valleys that make shadows. The unstitched areas are left to puff up, making little 'hills' which catch the light.

### QUILTING DESIGNS AND HOW THEY ARE MARKED
There are many ways of marking a pattern ready for quilting. You will need to select the method best suited to your project and the way in which you will quilt it. Different kinds of marking are done at different stages of the quilting, so take note of when to mark for your chosen method.

### KINDS OF QUILTING DESIGNS
1) Grid patterns
Patterns of lines are easy to mark and to quilt. Use a long ruler or a long, smooth, thin piece of wood to help you mark these designs. Marking grids for hand quilting may be done in pencil before the quilting layers are put together. Alternatively, for both hand and machine quilting, the marking can be done with chalk just before quilting.

## 2) Outline quilting

The patches in the blocks can be outlined with quilting. The outline quilting can be 'in the ditch', which means that the stitching is almost, but not quite, on top of the seam line. The quilting is always done on the side away from the seam allowances and needs no marking. Alternatively, outline quilting may be done at some little distance in from the seam line. For example, you may have the stitching 6 mm from the seam line. Narrow masking tape can be used to mark lines at an even distance alongside the seam line. Or, chalk lines could be ruled just prior to quilting.

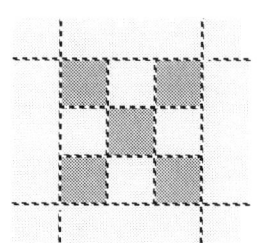

## 3) Quilting motifs and designs

Designs for quilting can be as varied as your imagination allows. Traditional designs include wreaths, twisted plaits, fans, hearts, knots, flowers, leaves, semi-circles and circles, but all kinds of shape and pattern are possible. There are many commercially available quilting designs and books full of patterns for you to copy. Designs can also be made by using shapes from wrought iron, ceiling patterns or any decorative form that appeals to you. These patterns must be marked with a pencil (for hand quilting) or chalk (for machine quilting).

## 4) Echo quilting

Quilting lines which echo a patchwork shape may be worked freely, without being marked. If straight lines are required, use pencil or chalk and a ruler.

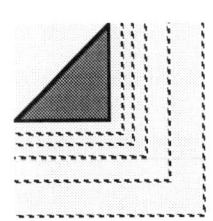

## 5) Free quilting

As the name suggests, free quilting describes lines which meander across the quilt. No marking is necessary, and the work can be done by hand or machine.

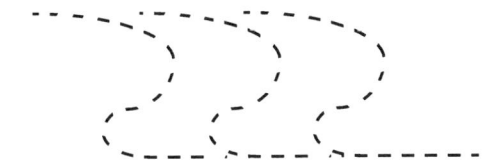

## METHODS OF MARKING

*Pencil:* Lightly drawn pencil lines are the best way of marking quilting designs for hand quilting. This kind of marking works best on light-coloured fabrics. Using a good quality, very sharp HB pencil, draw lines lightly so that no unsightly dark pencil lines will be left after the quilting is finished. Always keep the pencil sharp. Pencil marking is done *before* the layers of the quilt are put together. Stencils (either of plastic or cardboard) may be drawn around for quilting designs.

*Chalk:* Chalk pencils or powdered chalk dispensers (chalk wheels) are ideal for marking a quilt. The chalk brushes off easily leaving no unsightly marks. Chalk is available in several different colours. Because the lines disappear easily, chalk marking must be done *after* the layers are joined, just prior to quilting.

*Masking tape:* Masking tape is applied *after* the layers are joined. The tape should be put in place immediately before quilting. It should never be left on the quilt when you are not actually stitching. It can be used several times before it loses its stickiness.

## HAND QUILTING

The stitches in hand quilting form a gentle broken line that blends into the fabrics. Aim for neat and even stitches rather than tiny ones.

1. Layering a quilt ready for hand quilting

a) Prepare the fabric for the quilt backing by joining pieces as required to make a back 5—8 cm larger all around than the quilt top. For example, if the quilt top is 200 cm x 150 cm, the backing needs to be at least 210 cm x 160 cm. Press the backing and lay it out, right side down, on a large clear surface. Tape (with masking tape) or pin the backing down so that it is smooth but not tight. Use a large table or spread the quilt out on the floor.

b) Spread the batting on top of the backing, smoothing it gently in place. There should be no lumps, bumps or wrinkles.

If the batting needs to be joined, place the two edges neatly side by side and oversew by hand.

c) Press the quilt top and lay it on top of the batting, right side up.

d) Pin the layers of the quilt together. Then, using a long needle and long pieces of thread, tack (baste) the quilt layers together. Make a square grid of lines about 10—15 cm across the quilt.

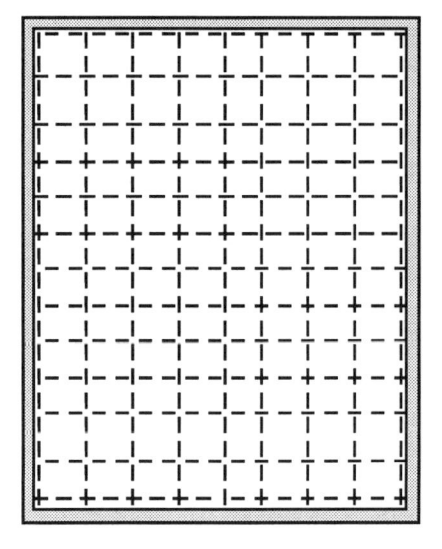

For large quilts, pin the layers together on the floor, then very carefully move the quilt to the largest table you can find for the tacking. Be careful that all the layers are even and smooth after you have spread it out on the table.

2. Placing the quilt in a hoop or frame

A quilting hoop or quilting frame holds the three layers of a quilt smoothly in place, leaving your hands free to quilt. The quilt should be placed carefully in a hoop or frame so that all the layers are flat and in place, without rumpling. The quilt should not be drum-tight.

3. The quilting stitch

The quilting stitch is just a simple running stitch, but it should be an even one and must go through all three layers of the quilt.

Prepare for quilting by setting yourself up with quilting thread, a 'between' quilting needle, a small pair of scissors and one or two thimbles (or other protection for your fingers). A thimble is worn on the third finger of the hand

## QUILT CONSTRUCTION

with which you hold the needle. If a second thimble or protector is used, it is placed on the second or third finger (whichever finger the needle grazes as it goes through the quilt) of your other hand.

Thread your needle and make a knot in the end of the thread. Working from the top of the quilt, decide where you will begin quilting. Make a stitch a centimetre or two long that comes out exactly where you have decided your first stitch will begin. Pull on the thread gently until the knot pops through the quilt top and lodges in the batting.

With one hand above the quilt and the other below, make small running stitches by first pushing the needle down vertically until it grazes your finger below the quilt. Then rock the needle so that its tip comes back up to the surface again. With practice, you'll find that you can take several stitches with this rocking motion. Check underneath your work occasionally to see that you are making stitches which go through all three layers. As you make this rocking action, the thimble on the hand holding the needle should be doing the pushing. The finger below the quilt is grazed by the needle as it penetrates the three layers; the needle is then guided back up again.

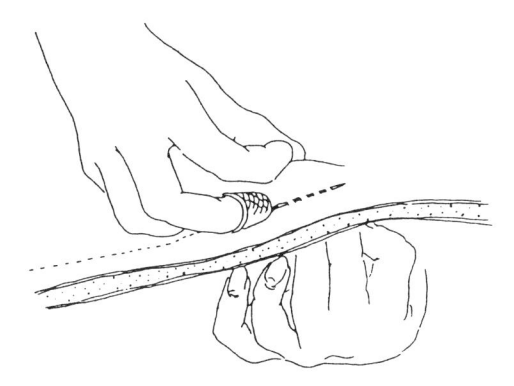

End the quilting by taking a small backstitch which is split. Then run the thread away into the batting and snip off the end.

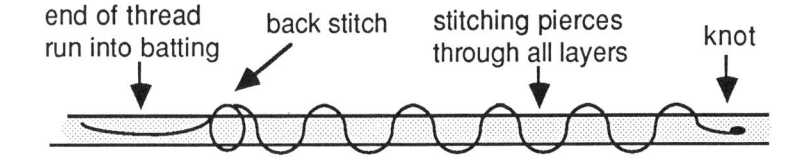

Side view, quilting

## MACHINE QUILTING

Machine quilting has a stronger, more unbroken line than hand quilting. However, if clear monofilament thread is used, the thread will blend into the colours of the fabric and create a softer line.

You may like to choose a firmer cotton as the backing for machine quilting than that which you would use for hand quilting. A firmer backing is less likely to stretch and bunch under the machine foot than a soft fabric. Use a pure cotton fabric for the backing; polyester fabrics may slide under the machine and make the quilting difficult. Generally, machine quilting is more successful with the thinner type of batting. Thinner batting fits more comfortably under the arm of the machine.

### 1. Layering a quilt ready for machine quilting

Follow the procedure for layering a quilt ready for hand quilting up to the point where the layers are all smoothly in place (as in step 3 above). But, instead of pinning and tacking the layers in place, pin them together with safety pins. You will need approximately 3 cm safety pins. Use a two-step process to do the pinning:

i) Put in all the pins, but do not close them. Put them in as if they were ordinary straight pins. Place pins about 10 cm apart, trying to avoid the places where you know the quilting lines will go.

ii) Check that all the layers are smooth, then close all the pins.

(The reason for this two-step operation is that the action of closing the pins might lift and rumple the layers.)

### 2. Setting up a space for machine quilting

It is very important to set up a big space around your machine for machine quilting. The larger the quilt, the larger the space needs to be. You want a smooth surface for the quilt to slide along both in front and behind the machine. If you can, set up an extra table beside and to the left of you as you sit at your machine. This will support the weight of the quilt as it is fed through the machine. At no stage do you want the quilt to drop over the edge of the table, or it will drag through the machine. If you only have a small table for the machine, set yourself up against a wall — the quilt will bunch up against it, but it will be prevented from falling over the edge.

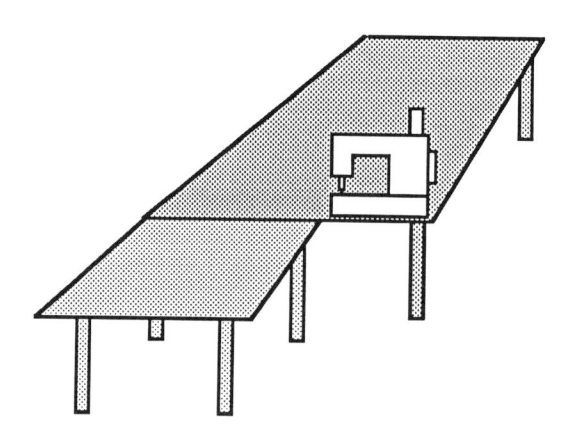

Set up your machine for flat-bed stitching; a large space around the needle is an advantage in helping you smooth the quilt in front of the needle.

## 3. Packaging the quilt ready for machining

Machine quilting is limited by the amount of space which you have under the arm of the machine. A large quilt will need to be rolled or folded neatly so that it will fit under the arm. Your main aim is to see that the quilt goes through the machine as smoothly as possible.

For large quilts which are to be quilted in lines from edge to edge, you'll need to roll the quilt up firmly from the side going under the machine arm. The other side can be folded or loosely rolled, leaving a long corridor of space down the middle where you will be doing the quilting. The rolled and folded quilt can then be loosely refolded in the opposite direction so that is fits on the table beside you. As you sew the quilt, you will need to stop from time to time to rearrange it to ensure the next section is ready to move smoothly.

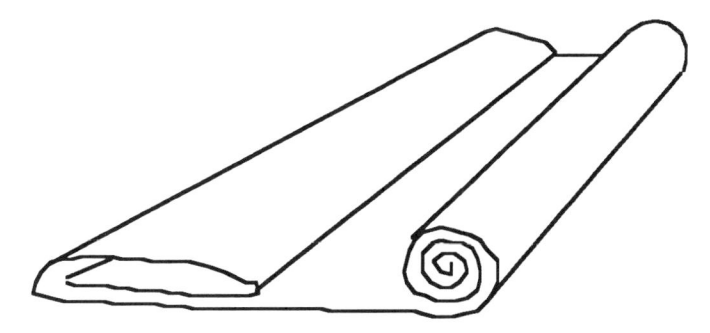

## 4. The process of machine quilting

Machine quilting can be done either with ordinary dressmaking thread (in a colour which will match or blend into the colour of the quilt top), or it can be done with a clear monofilament thread which will blend into all colours. Thread the bobbin with thread that matches the backing fabric. (Do not use monofilament thread on the bobbin.)

Begin and end your line of quilting either with 0.5 cm very tiny stitching (put the stitch length down to very low), or else backtrack a few stitches. Feed the quilt through the machine as smoothly as possible. When you need to stop stitching in order to rearrange the quilt, make sure you stop with the needle in the down position so there are no jumps in the line of stitching. If you are quilting in the ditch, sew close to the seam line, but keeping to the side away from the seam allowances. Finish off the thread ends either by snipping them off, or by sewing them into the batting.

As you are sewing, smooth the section of the quilt just in front of the needle by spreading the second and third fingers of your left hand just in front of the machine foot.

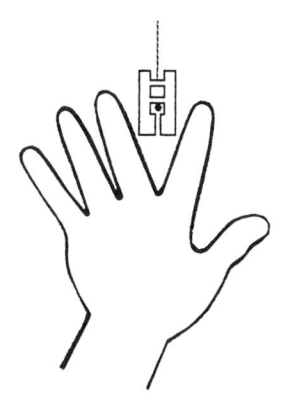

The quilt may seem very big and unmanageable. But if it is properly pinned, you will find that, if you concentrate on keeping the section just in front of the needle smooth, the rest of the quilt will look after itself.

For a large quilt quilted from side to side, begin stitching in the centre and work your way across to the edge or corner. Turn the quilt around and re-roll it from the other side and work your way across to the opposite edge or corner. To make a grid, repeat the same procedures in the other direction. You may find it easier to do this cross-stitching with all the pins removed.

Machine quilting in any and all directions can be done on small quilts up to the size of about 1.5 m x 1.5 m, provided the quilt is well pinned. Beyond this, the quilt becomes too unmanageable to turn around corners. It must be quilted in a grid pattern of lines which go from one side of the quilt to the other. Or free machine quilting can be done by dropping the feed dogs, putting the darning foot on your machine and moving a small part of the quilt under the needle.

For free machine quilting, the quilt must be firmly rolled up, so that only the space where you are working is open for stitching. To set up the machine, follow the directions for darning in your machine booklet. Mastering free machine quilting with the feed dogs down requires practice; you have to move the quilt smoothly so the stitches remain even. Get to grips with the skills before you start a big quilt.

Another alternative for large quilts is to construct and machine quilt them in pieces, and then to join the pieces. If machine quilting goes right up to the edges being joined, stitch all layers of the quilt together, right sides facing. Trim away excess batting and seam allowances. Then, cover the seam allowances with straight-grain strips of fabric, with edges folded and pressed under. Hand stitch the strips in place.

If there is no quilting at the edges to be joined, stitch five of the layers together, leaving out the backing layer on one side. Trim away excess batting and seam allowances. Fold a seam allowance under on the loose backing, lap over the seam and hand sew in place.

### Binding

Binding finishes the edges of a completed quilt. The finished width of the binding can be varied to suit the design. Usually, the strips are cut so that the binding can be put on doubled, which makes a good firm edge. The width you require to do this is calculated as four times the width of the finished binding, plus 1.5 cm for seam allowances. For example, for a finished binding 1 cm wide, cut the strips 5.5 cm wide.

Strips for binding are usually cut on the straight grain. However bias-grain strips can be used if preferred, or if the binding has to be put on rounded corners. Join strips to make the lengths required, then fold them in half lengthwise and press.

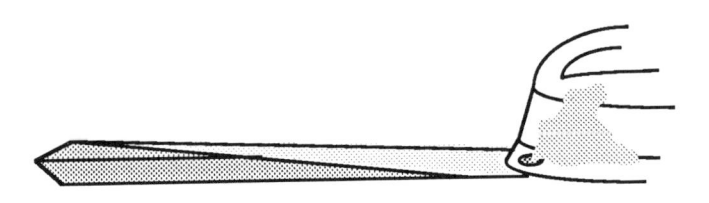

# QUILT CONSTRUCTION

As discussed in the method for adding borders, it's important to measure the quilt first through its centre to find the exact length required for the binding strips. Pin-mark the length required rather than cutting it; this will give you a little leeway in the sewing. Working on the sides of the quilt first, pin-mark the quilt and the binding strips at their centres. Pin the binding to the right side of the quilt, matching the pin-marks. Pin-mark in quarters for a large quilt. Stitch the binding in place. Pin the binding to the back of the quilt at each corner. Repeat the process for the binding at the top and bottom of the quilt, stitching across the folded binding at the corner to the edge of the quilt.

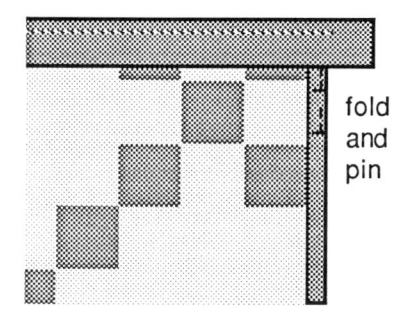

fold and pin

Pin and hand stitch the binding in place, tucking it neatly around the corners.

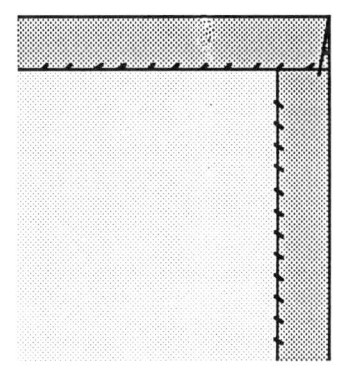

Corners of the binding may be mitred, if preferred. In this case, stitch the binding to a corner of the quilt only, not into the seam allowances. Working on each corner separately, fold and stitch the mitres by hand. Alternatively, fold and stitch corners by machine, following the procedure for mitring border corners (see p. 51), but make a right-angle in the drawn line on which you will be stitching.

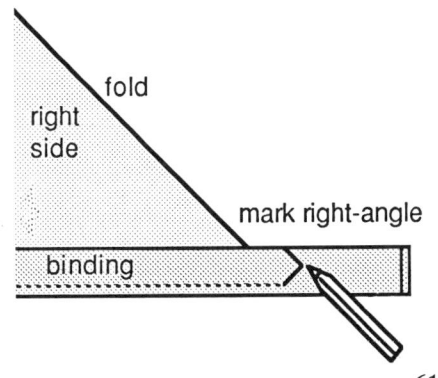

## THE FINAL TOUCHES — A SLEEVE AND A LABEL

If your quilt is to hang in an exhibition or on a wall at home, add a sleeve to the top of the back of the quilt. Using the backing fabric, cut a strip 22 cm wide. Its length will be the measurement from one side of the quilt to the other. Hem each end, then fold the strip in half lengthwise, right sides together. Sew to make a tube. Turn right side out and press. Hand sew in place, just beneath the binding at the back of the quilt.

If preferred, the folded strip of fabric (with hemmed ends) can be sewn to the quilt by machine after the binding has been machine-sewn — but before the binding has been hand stitched in place. Hand stitch the folded side in place.

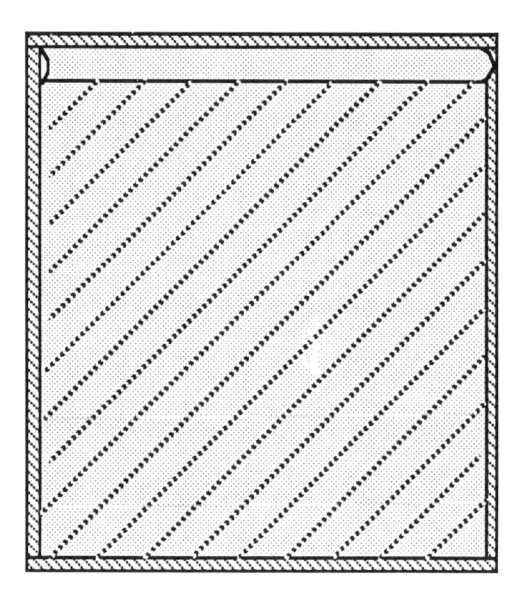

Sleeve

Make labels for your work from small rectangles of fabric. Hand embroidery, fabric pens or machine-sewn lettering (available on some computerised sewing machines) can be used to 'write' the title of the quilt, your name, the date and any other message you wish. A border of decorative machine stitching would be an attractive finish. Alternatively, embroider your name on the front or back of the quilt.

Your descendants will thank you for taking the extra time to add this final touch. Don't contribute to 'anonymous' being a woman!

"SUMMER ROSES"
MARGARET ROLFE
1993

Label

# DESIGNING A QUILT

**D**esigning may sound a scary word, but all it means is that you are making choices. When you have chosen a block design, decided how you will repeat and arrange it, and then selected the fabrics, you have designed a quilt. The important thing is to be conscious of the choices you are making, so that you explore the possibilities before you arrive at each decision.

### CHOOSING A BLOCK DESIGN

The first step in creating a quilt is to choose which block design to make. While there are hundreds and hundreds of block designs to choose from, this book features a selection, each of which is easy to make using the rotary cutter. The blocks are all combinations of simple shapes — the square, the rectangle, the half-square triangle and the quarter-square triangle.

UNDERSTANDING THE 'PATCH' SYSTEM
Quilters often become concerned because they believe they must have an exact pattern for a particular block. However, patchwork blocks should be seen not so much as individual designs, but rather as part of a system capable of endless variations. Once you understand the system, lots of possibilities will open up for you — not only for using existing block designs, but also for manipulating the blocks in your own way.

The system is based on groups of squares. The secret in analysing a block is to imagine how a grid of squares will fit neatly onto it. For example, if you look at an Ohio Star block, you can see that a group of nine squares arranged in three rows of three will fit neatly over it. So, the block is a 9-patch because it can have a grid of 3 x 3 squares neatly fitted on to it. However, if you tried to impose a grid of 4 x 4 squares on the Ohio Star, it would not fit exactly. So, the block is not a 4-patch.

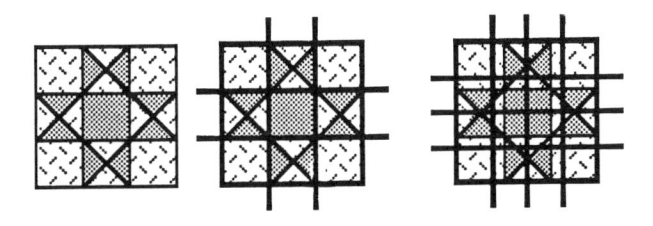

Using the Sawtooth Star block as another example, the grid of 4 x 4 squares fits neatly, while the grid of 3 x 3 squares does not. So, the Sawtooth Star is a 4-patch block.

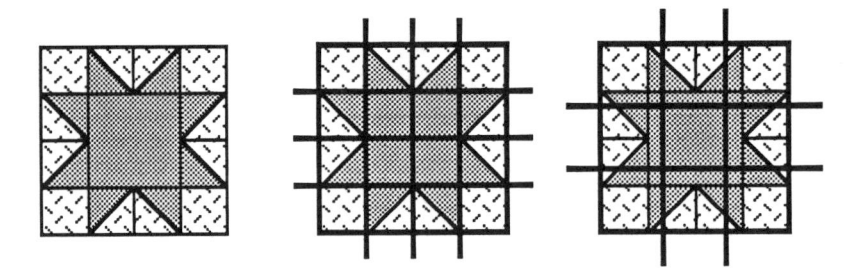

The squares in this patchwork system are called 'patches'. The blocks are named *either* according to how many squares (or patches) are in each block (as in 9-patch), *or* they are named according to how many sets of rows of patches are in the block (as in 5-patch). Although the system is completely logical, the numbers used for the patches are not quite as logical. However, once you understand the concept behind the system, it all makes sense.

Once you can determine how many patches there are in a particular block, you are able to decide how big these patches should be. From this you will be able to work out easily the sizes of all the shapes in the block. Add the appropriate seam allowances to these shapes and you can cut out the block. For example, if you have a 4-patch block, such as the Road to Oklahoma, you could decide to make each patch 7 cm finished size. Therefore, the block will be 28 cm square; you will cut the squares 8.5 cm and the half-square triangles from 9.5 cm squares.

**The 9-patch block**
The most well-known patchwork block is the simple Nine-patch — a block containing nine patches, as its name suggests.

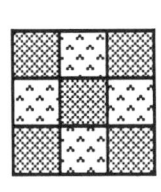

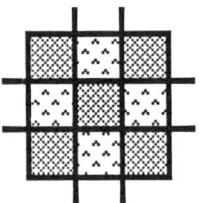

The nine patches are arranged in three rows of three squares each. On the basis of this, all blocks which have three rows of three patches have come to be called 9-patch blocks. Note that in this book the block called Nine-patch will be differentiated from the general class of blocks called 9-patch by giving the block the name with the nine in letters (Nine-patch), and the class of patches with the nine as a number (9-patch).

Any block which can have a grid of 3 x 3 squares imposed on top of it is called a 9-patch.

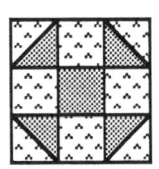

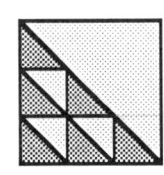

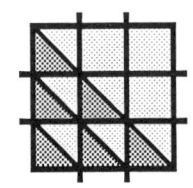

# DESIGNING A QUILT

Note that some of these blocks may have further subdivisions within the nine squares.

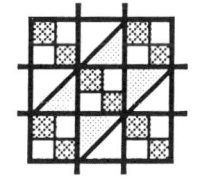

For a selection of 9-patch blocks, see p. 80—85.

## The 4-patch block

The next class of blocks is called 4-patch. Again, these blocks take their name from the Four-patch block which is a block comprising four equal squares.

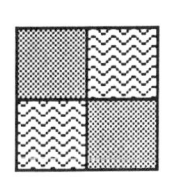

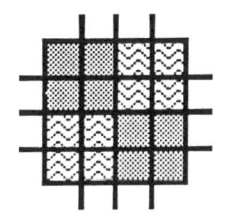

While strictly speaking the Four-patch block has a grid of 2 x 2 squares imposed on it, the term 4-patch has come to be used for all blocks onto which a grid of 4 x 4 squares can be imposed. Of course, a four-square grid will also fit neatly onto the 2 x 2 square arrangement of the Four-patch, so there is no difficulty with this terminology. Note that as for Nine-patch blocks, in this book the individual block called the Four-patch is identified with the four in letters, while the class of blocks divisible by four is called 4-patch with the four as a number.

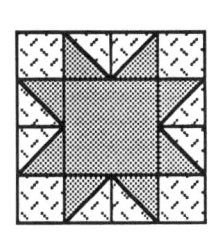

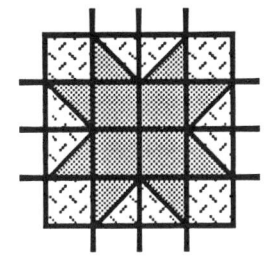

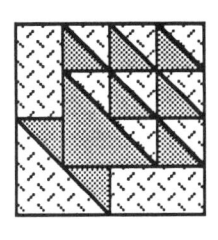

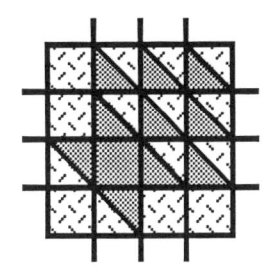

Again, some of these blocks may have even further subdivisions within the squares. For a selection of 4-patch blocks, see p. 86—98.

## The 5-patch block

The 5-patch blocks are those which can have a grid of 5 x 5 squares imposed on them.

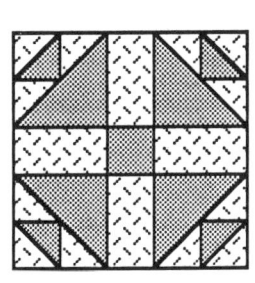

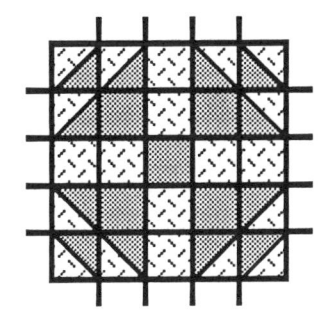

For a selection of 5-patch blocks, see p. 98—102.

**The 7-patch block**
The 7-patch blocks are those which can have a grid of 7 x 7 squares imposed on them.

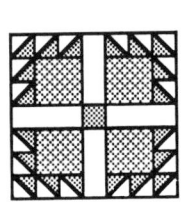

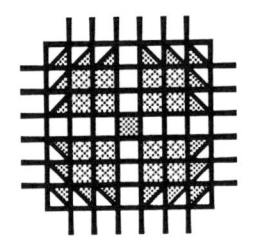

For a selection of 7-patch blocks, see p. 102—104.

**1-patch patchwork designs**
1-patch quilt designs are made by repeating only one shape. Patterns are still formed, but they are not necessarily block patterns. This book only illustrates 1-patch designs which are easy to rotary cut, such as the square, the half-square triangle and the rectangle.

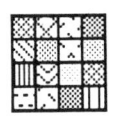

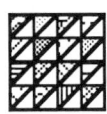

There are many other popular 1-patch designs such as the hexagon and the diamond created by the hexagon, but as these shapes are not possible to make easily using rotary-cutting techniques, they have not been included.

**Other blocks**
Besides the 9-patch, 4-patch, 5-patch, 7-patch blocks and 1-patch designs, there are other pieced block designs not covered in this book because their shapes do not lend themselves easily to rotary cutting. Examples of such designs are all the 8-pointed star blocks and other block designs based on an octagon, such as Kaleidoscope. If you try to apply the patch system to a block and find it does not work, chances are that you may have one of these blocks.

### CHOOSING A QUILT SET

The 'set' of a quilt refers to the way in which the patchwork blocks are joined to make the quilt top, that is, before any borders or binding are added. There are many possibilities. What follows is an illustrated guide to the most common ways of arranging blocks.

ADJACENT BLOCKS
All the blocks are sewn next to each other. Watch for interesting secondary patterns created by the juxtaposition of the blocks.

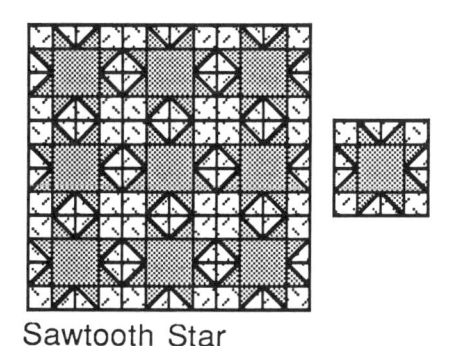

# DESIGNING A QUILT

Sawtooth Star

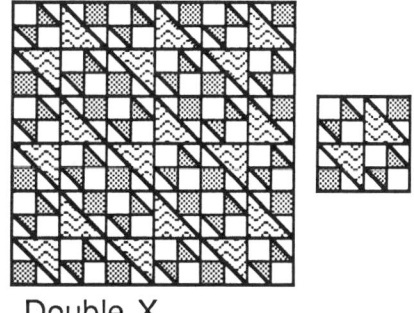

Double X

Interesting secondary patterns may also be created deliberately by rotating some of the adjacent blocks. This works when blocks have a diagonal direction to them.

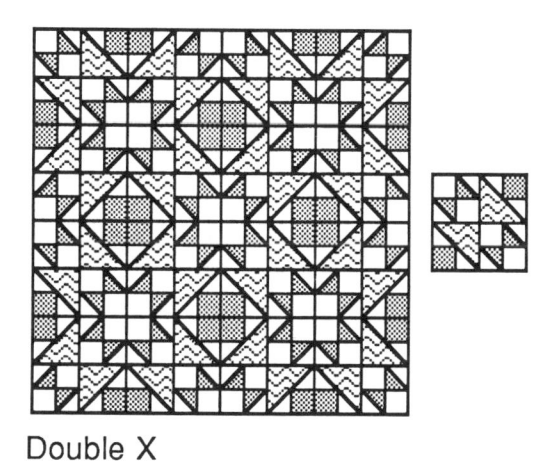

Double X

## ALTERNATE PLAIN BLOCKS
Every alternate block is plain. The plain blocks offer an excellent space for quilting designs and can also give the eye a 'rest' from busy blocks. Another alternative is to use a special print in the alternate blocks.

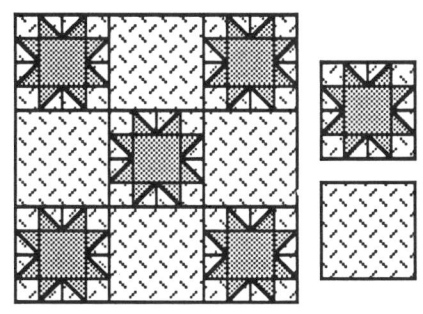

Sawtooth Star
Plain block

## ALTERNATE PIECED BLOCKS

Two different blocks may be combined to make interesting patterns. There are two main ways of doing this: either combine two blocks, or design a very simple block for the alternate block.

1) Combining two traditional blocks.

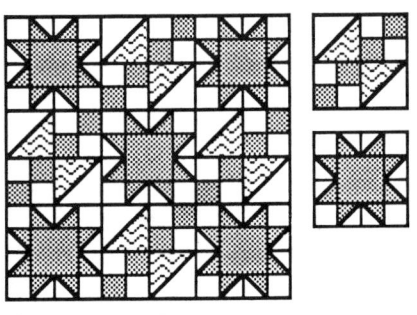

**Sawtooth Star and Buckeye Beauty**

2) Designing a simple pattern which will combine well with the main block design. These blocks can be called 'connector blocks' because they connect the blocks in an interesting way, even though, in themselves, they may be quite simple.

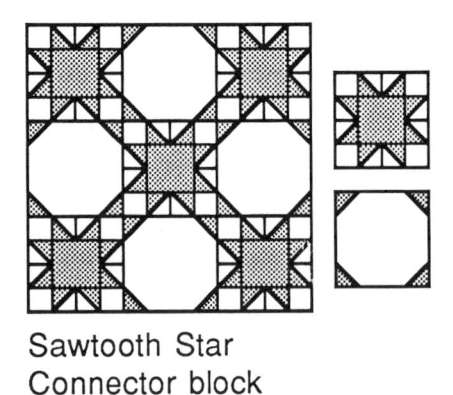

**Sawtooth Star Connector block**

One way of designing such a block is to repeat the main one, but omit some parts of the design.

# DESIGNING A QUILT

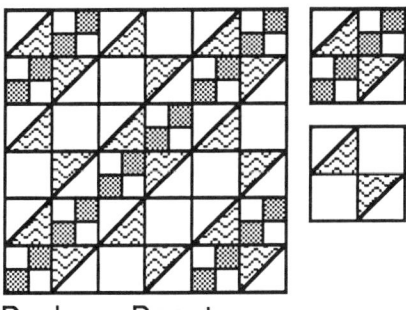

**Buckeye Beauty Connector block**

## SASHING BETWEEN BLOCKS
Sashing refers to the strips of fabric sewn between blocks to create a 'frame'. Sashing can vary in width to produce different effects.

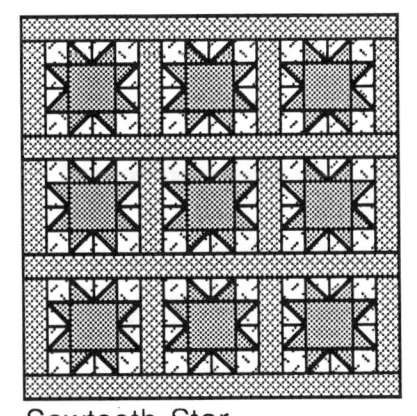

**Sawtooth Star**

## PIECED SASHING BETWEEN BLOCKS
The sashing strips between blocks may be pieced. The most common way to do this is to place squares (sometimes called 'posts') in the corners of the blocks.

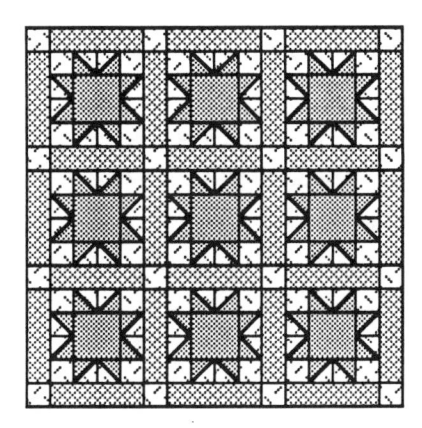

More elaborate piecing is also possible, especially if the sashing is wide.

### BLOCKS INTO STRIPS
The blocks may be arranged into strips to create strongly horizontal or vertical designs.

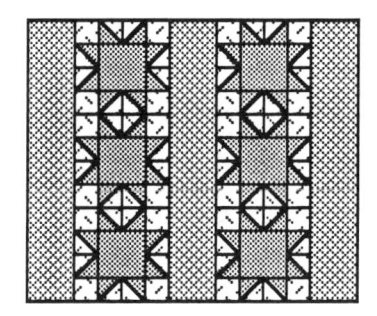

### MEDALLION ARRANGEMENT
The medallion style of making a quilt involves working a design from the centre outwards. The centre can be formed from a single block or a group of blocks, or may even be a plain or printed piece of fabric. This centre, which acts as the focal point of the quilt design, is then surrounded by successive borders. These borders can be simply strips of fabric, pieced border designs, or further block designs.

## DIAGONAL SETS

Blocks can be rotated by 45°. This is sometimes described as having the blocks 'on point'. The squares of the blocks then form diamonds. All of the previously mentioned ways of arranging the blocks (adjacent blocks, alternate plain blocks, alternate pieced blocks, sashing between blocks, blocks into strips and the medallion arrangement) can be used with the blocks placed on point. Note that triangles will form at the edges and at the corners of the quilt.

### CHOOSING BORDERS

Most quilts are enhanced by a border or borders framing the centre of the design. Another advantage is that borders are an easy, quick way to increase the size of a quilt, particularly if you need to make adjustments so that it can fit a different size of bed.

Borders can be made from strips of fabric, multiple strips of fabric or further patchwork. This in turn can be as simple as squares added in the corners, or take a more elaborate form such as a pieced border or further blocks. Squared or mitred corners are both possible, depending on which best suits the style of the quilt and the fabrics used. Quilts with the blocks on point usually look better with mitred corners because they follow the diagonal lines of the blocks. Border prints usually require mitred corners, so that the print in the borders meets at the corners.

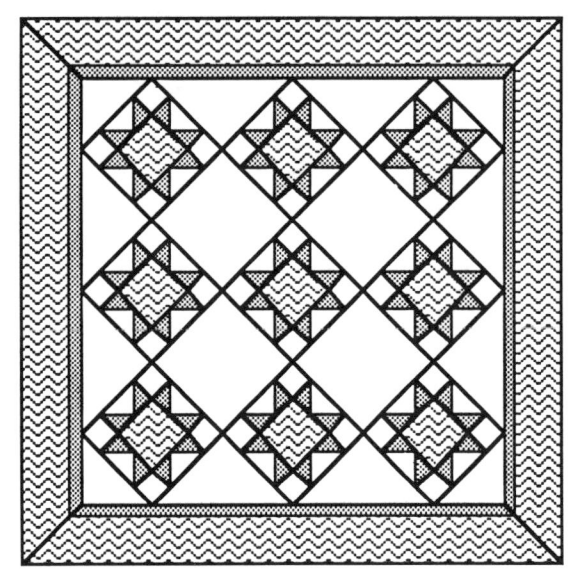

While border fabrics can be chosen at the outset of quilt making, often it is better to wait until the centre is finished. Then select a border which will enhance the overall look. Special border prints can often be used to great effect, or large prints may perform a similar role.

### Choosing your fabrics

There are three important dimensions in choosing fabrics: tonal value, colour and pattern.

1. Tonal value

Tonal value refers to the lightness or darkness of a fabric. At first glance, this may seem straightforward; some fabrics are easily labelled dark, others light. In fact, it is not quite as easy as that. Usually, the lightness or darkness of any one fabric is determined by the lightness or darkness of the fabrics next to it. A mid-tone fabric could be called dark if it is placed next to lighter fabrics. But it could also be seen as light when placed with something darker. Only pure white and pure black can categorically be called light and dark. All other fabrics can be arranged to be either light or dark, depending on how they react to their neighbours.

### Dark to light

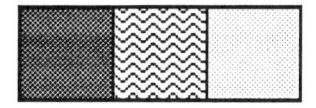

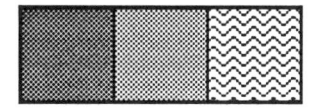

Dark to medium - medium becomes light

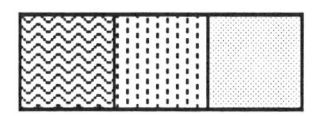

Medium to light - medium becomes dark

Think of your fabrics as social creatures. Always consider how they are going to get along with the ones next door.

You can determine the tonal value of your fabrics by looking at them from a distance. Try to view them from as far away as possible. In small spaces, you can use some mechanical aids to help you see the fabrics as if they were at a distance: backwards through a pair of binoculars; through a camera; through a peephole for a door (an inexpensive device from hardware shops); through a 'reducing' glass — the opposite of a magnifying glass.

Tonal value is the most important consideration when choosing fabrics, more important even than colour. Why? Because it is the tonal values that ultimately create the design of the quilt. If all your tonal values are too similar, you will find you will lose the pattern, even though the colours themselves are widely different.

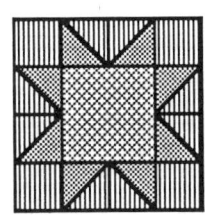

Tonal value creates the design

Different effects can be created depending on how you handle tonal values. For example, a strong contrast in tonal values leads to bold designs; a subtle shift in tonal values results in a softer effect. Try to imagine your quilt in a black and white photograph — how would it look?

## 2. Colour

Colour is the most appealing aspect of a quilt. Usually we fall in love with one because we're attracted to its colour.

Don't feel obliged to follow any so-called 'rules' about colour. What you choose should reflect your own taste — and everyone's taste is different. But having some appreciation of the way colours work, and especially how they interact, can make your choices more successful. Remember that colours not only make an impact by themselves, they are also affected by others around them. Have you ever admired a red, red rose? The redness of the rose is actually enhanced by the green leaves which surround it, because red and green contrast. Blue next to a green will make the blue look more blue, and the green look more green.

Once again, think of your fabrics in terms of the company they keep. Are they getting along well with their neighbours, or are they clashing loudly? To gain a particular effect, you may choose to have them clashing with each other, but you must be in control of the effect you want to make.

When planning a quilt, always try to group your fabrics so that you get a clear picture of how they will interact.

## 3. Pattern

The fabric pattern is another consideration when making your selection. The pattern may be printed or may be woven (plaids and stripes, for example). Or there may be no pattern at all, as with solid-colour fabrics.

Ideally, you should choose a group of patterns which vary in scale, density and design. For example, a quilt made entirely of small prints can look overly busy and fussy, while one featuring solely large prints can be overwhelming. But combinations of small and large, geometric and floral, random and regimented, sparse and dense prints, can create great visual interest. Stripes and checks can add tremendous vitality to a quilt design, so don't overlook them.

## GETTING IT ALL TOGETHER

So what does this all mean when you are in a quilt shop and faced with an enticing array of fabrics in all colours of the rainbow, with beautiful prints at every turn?

A practical approach to choosing colours for a quilt is to first choose a fabric you love, and then to build around it. After all, the work of very talented textile designers is readily available to you, so why not tap into their skills?

Once you have selected your key fabric, identify all the colours you can find within it, then select other fabrics that will complement your original choice. Try to group the fabrics to see how they interact. Always keep in mind the variables of tonal value and pattern, and be sure to have a variety in your selection.

The more fabrics there are in a quilt, the less any single one of them matters. But the fewer the fabrics, the more important it is that your choices are the right ones. Remember, too, that the odd piece of fabric which seems ugly by itself may be perfectly appropriate in your quilt when viewed in overall context.

Beware, though, of over-matching. You can choose a group of fabrics which go together so well that they generate not a spark of vitality — you may as well have just chosen one print. Add a note of vibrancy, or something a bit unexpected. Your quilt will be much stronger for it.

## CHOOSING FABRICS FOR SCRAP QUILTS

Scrap quilts have enduring charm, but there are some important principles to keep in mind to ensure yours is a success. Some people think that making a scrap quilt means they can use anything and everything in their fabric collection. The opposite is the case. The most impressive scrap quilts rely for their impact on carefully considered use of colour. 'Good bones', in other words a good structure, are what count. Two things create this structure — the tonal values and the colour range.

### 1. Tonal values

These are important for all quilts, but often it is solely the tonal values — the lights and darks — which create the pattern for a scrap quilt. However, within those lights and darks, there should be variation. No matter what the colours, if all the darks are equally dark, and all the lights equally light, the result can be boring. You may find that you can use a mid-tone fabric in both the dark and light areas of one quilt. Look at the Summer Roses quilt (see p. 105), and you'll appreciate the effect made by the variation of tonal values in both dark and light areas.

### 2. Colour selection

Scrap quilts are much improved if some thought is given to the 'theme' of the colours selected. For instance, the Summer Roses quilt (see colour pages) was based on two colours — blue and rose pink, and fabrics were then chosen which related to them. However, it was important to extend the palette by introducing various shades of blue and rose pink.

Sometimes a special fabric can become a strong feature, such as the large rose print in Summer Roses. This fabric also reflected exactly the colours of the original quilt plan — blue and rose pink. Always establish some criteria in the colours you choose; then extend these colours to create interest and variety. For example, in the Lady of the Lake quilt (see p. 114), red and blue fabrics were chosen, but the reds vary from rust, cherry red and maroon to reddish-purple.

Adding some patches of brighter colour will enliven your quilt. Note the vitality generated by the bright electric blues and hot pink patches in the Lady of the Lake quilt (see colour pages).

### CREATING AN EXCITING QUILT DESIGN

Some beautifully made quilts, containing lovely colours and fabrics can, nevertheless, seem rather dull. They lack a certain something that is hard, at first, to pinpoint.

A concept to keep in mind is that a good quilt should be worth a second look. If you study many of the much-admired antique quilts, you'll find that after you register their initial impact, they will 'unfold', revealing a pattern, or patterns, other than the main one. Often, two blocks together create this effect, such as the secondary star design in the centre of the Ohio Star quilt (see colour pages).

There is a physiological basis for this phenomenon because our eyes can only see one pattern at a time. It is the old faces/vase conundrum — you can either see the vase, or you can see the face, but you cannot see both at the same time. This does much to explain why secondary patterns create such interest; your eye does not see them at first, but has to 're-look' to find them.

Other features which create interest are variations of tone and colour. No wonder we find scrap quilts fascinating; our eyes can rove over them for a long time, taking in the variety of the fabrics and how they work together to form the pattern. A good border can be another important source of interest, especially if it is pieced or utilises a novel fabric design.

Always remember that your eye likes to find patterns and order, but it also enjoys the break in the pattern, the contrasting element. Balancing both order and disorder, pattern and variation, is what you should be aiming for. A quilt should not be entirely predictable — your eye should delight in making new discoveries.

SUMMER ROSES QUILT, DESIGNED AND MADE BY MARGARET ROLFE
Machine pieced and hand quilted.
Finished quilt top measures 252 cm x 252 cm.

COUNTRY CHECKS QUILT, DESIGNED AND MADE BY JUDY TURNER
Machine pieced and machine quilted.
Finished quilt top measures 232 cm x 160 cm.

BEAR'S PAW QUILT, DESIGNED AND MADE BY BERYL HODGES
Machine pieced and machine quilted.
Finished quilt top measures 165 cm x 165 cm.

LADY OF THE LAKE QUILT, DESIGNED AND MADE BY MARGARET ROLFE
Machine pieced and machine quilted.
Finished quilt top measures 230 cm x 184 cm.

MARCHING GEESE QUILT, DESIGNED AND MADE BY BERYL HODGES
Machine pieced and machine quilted.
Finished quilt top measures 122 cm x 122 cm.

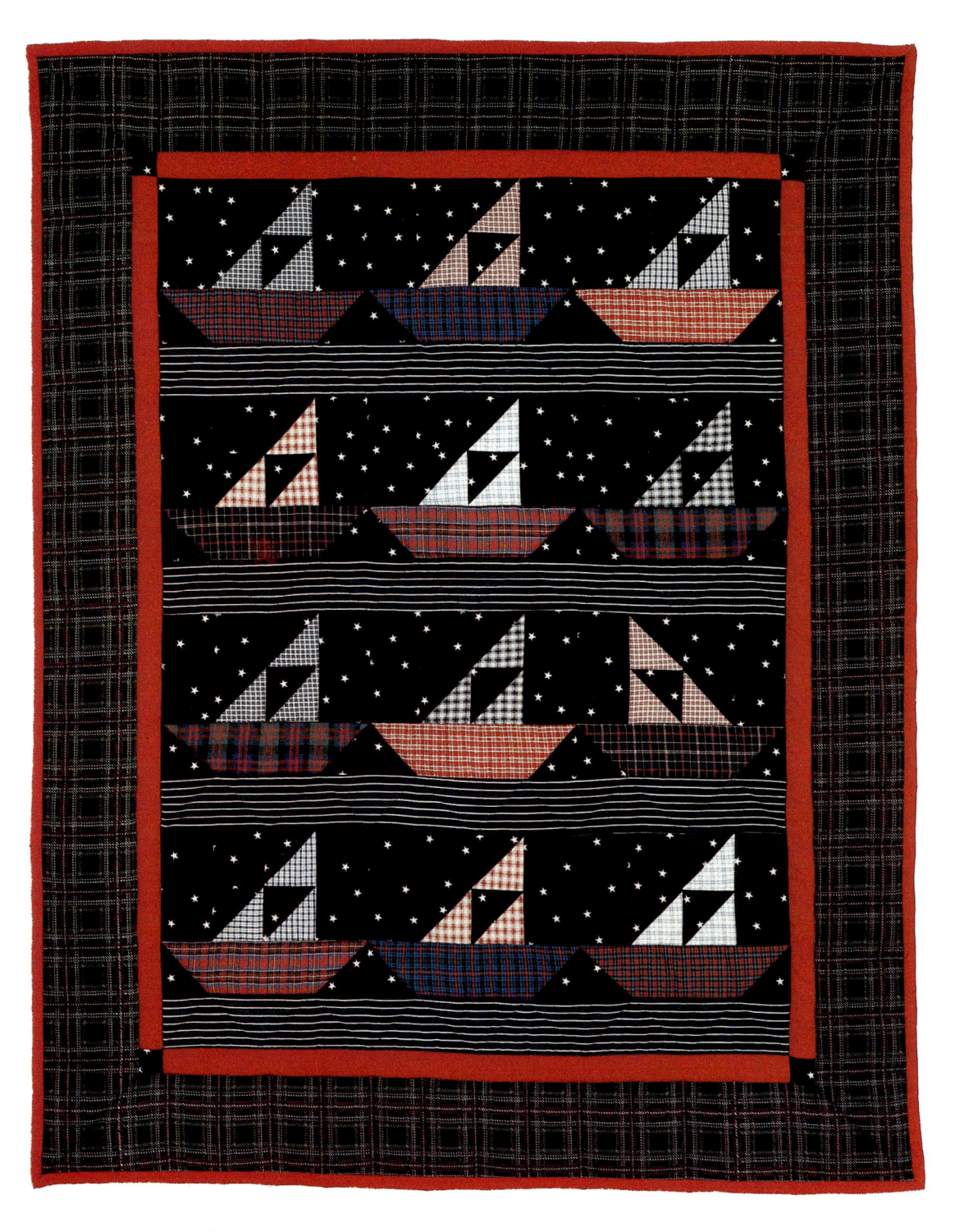

SAILING SHIPS QUILT, DESIGNED AND MADE BY BERYL HODGES
Machine pieced and machine quilted.
Finished quilt top measures 105 cm x 85 cm.

VIBRANT STARS QUILT, DESIGNED AND PIECED BY MARGARET ROLFE,
QUILTED BY JUDY TURNER
Machine pieced and machine quilted.
Finished quilt top measures 180 cm x 132 cm.

OHIO STAR QUILT, DESIGNED AND PIECED BY MARGARET ROLFE,
QUILTED BY BETH MILLER
Machine pieced and hand quilted.
Finished quilt top measures 98 cm x 98 cm.

# PATCHWORK SHAPES AND BLOCK DESIGNS

**P**resented here is a selection of patchwork shapes and block designs which use simple shapes you can cut easily with your rotary cutter. Most of the best-known and best-loved classic quilt blocks are included.

The blocks are given the names by which they are most commonly known, but remember that there is nothing definitive about quilt block names. One block may have several names, and different blocks may be known by the one title. Colour and tonal value can change the appearance of a block, so a design may sometimes appear to be different when, in fact, it is not.

After each block design, a list of useful sizes is given. Note that this is the **finished block** size — the size it will be when it is incorporated into a quilt. It does not include seam allowances.

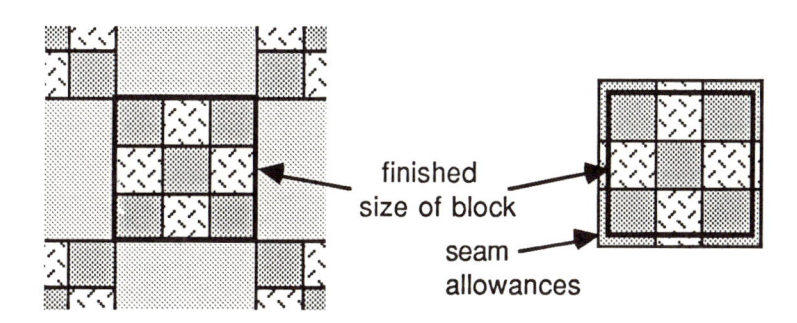

If you want to combine several block designs in one quilt, choose a size which will give you plenty of options. For example, a 24 cm block will allow you to use both 4-patch and 9-patch blocks. Using a 30 cm block will allow you to use 9-patch and 5-patch blocks, as well as 4-patch blocks if you make the size of the square 7.5 cm.

Also included in the information on each block is the size you need to cut the various shapes in the block. The sizes for the cut shapes will have the 0.75 cm seams included in the measurement.

Each block is given with a letter or letters indicating the shape or shapes in the block. All other parts of the block will be made up of the same shapes, although some of these may be turned around a different way. Even if this is the case, you still only need to cut out the same shape — the turning around occurs when you lay out the block before you begin to sew it together.

The blocks are shown divided into the shapes which make up the particular block design, but you should be aware that there may be other ways to cut out the shapes in the block to arrive at that same design. The way that the block divides into shapes is not necessarily definitive; some of the shapes may be either combined or split up, resulting in the same appearance, but requiring different shapes for cutting. For example, the Sawtooth Star may be cut using four quarter-square triangles between the points of the star, rather than the eight half-square triangles shown here. The ease of cutting strip-pieced half-square triangles makes it desirable to use these shapes where possible, but the choice is yours and is dependent on the needs of your particular project. Presented here is only one way of cutting out the shapes to make the block design. Remember, though, it is best to avoid having bias grain along the edges of a block because the bias grain stretches. Keep the edges of a block on the straight grain, if possible.

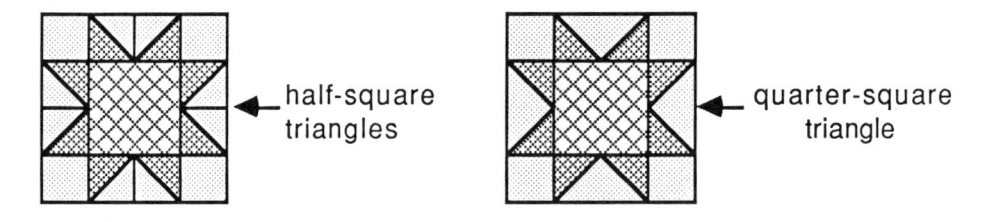

◄— half-square triangles

◄— quarter-square triangle

While this list of blocks gives a selection of sizes, you can make the blocks any size you want. This is done by determining the size of the squares (the patches) you want in the block then multiplying this by the number of squares necessary. (Each block is shown with the grid of squares superimposed on it — and for an explanation of the squares, see understanding the patch system, p. 63.) For example, if you decide to have 8.5 cm square in a 9-patch, the block size would be 25.5 cm x 25.5 cm. Alternatively, if the square in the block is 8.5 cm for a 4-patch design, then the block size would be 34 cm x 34 cm.

### 1-PATCH

1-patch is the name given to quilts made up of only one shape. The shapes do not usually form block designs, although the colours and tonal values chosen will still make patterns.

### SQUARE

The squares can be any size desired. Cut out the squares in

# PATCHWORK SHAPES AND BLOCK DESIGNS

the size required plus 1.5 cm. For example, for an 8 cm square (finished size), cut squares 9.5 cm square.

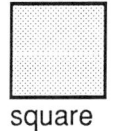

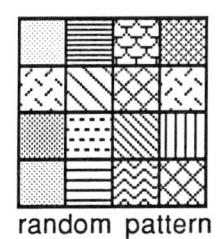

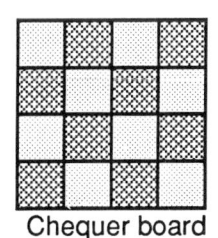

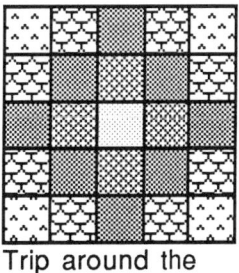

square

random pattern

Chequer board

Trip around the world

## HALF-SQUARE TRIANGLE

The half-square triangles may be made in any size. Half-square triangles are cut from a square, and the square should be the size of the shorter sides of the triangle, plus 2.5 cm for seam allowances (see p. 27). Each square yields two triangles when cut in half across the diagonal. For example, for a triangle which is half of an 8 cm square (finished size), cut a square which is 10.5 cm x 10.5 cm. Recut the square diagonally to make two half-square triangles. Half-square triangles can also be made quickly and accurately using a strip-pieced method (see p. 28).

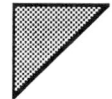

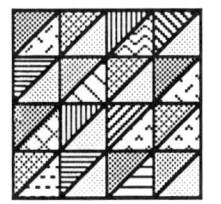

half-square triangle

Flying geese arrangement

Barn raising arrangement

## RECTANGLE

The rectangle may be cut to any size. Rectangles are cut the finished size plus 1.5 cm for the seam allowances. For example, an 8 cm x 16 cm rectangle (finished size) would be cut 9.5 cm x 17.5 cm.

rectangle

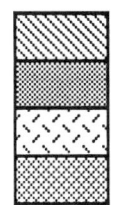

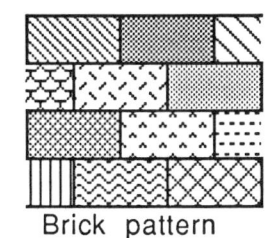

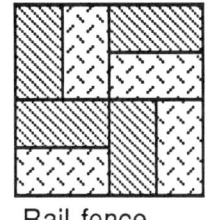

Brick pattern

Rail fence
(2 rectangles per square)

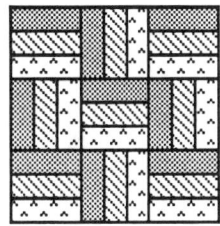

Rail fence
(3 rectangles per square)

## 9-PATCH — 3 X 3 SQUARES

9-patch blocks are those which can have a grid of 3 x 3 squares imposed on them. Choose block sizes which are multiples of three, such as 15 cm, 24 cm, 30 cm and 36 cm.

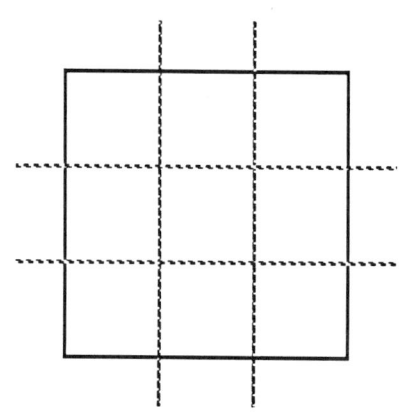

NINE-PATCH

- 15 cm block (3 x 3 squares, each 5 cm)
  Cut square A 6.5 cm square
- 18 cm block (3 x 3 squares, each 6 cm)
  Cut square A 7.5 cm square
- 24 cm block (3 x 3 squares, each 8 cm)
  Cut square A 9.5 cm square
- 30 cm block (3 x 3 squares, each 10 cm)
  Cut square A 11.5 cm square

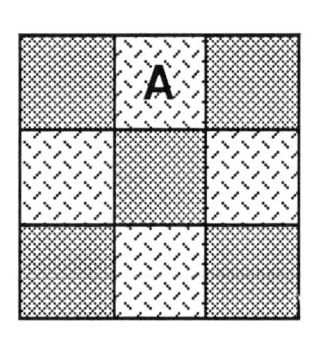

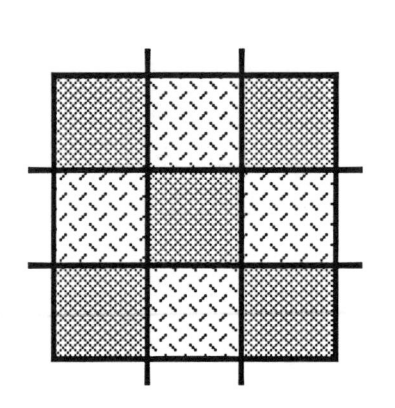

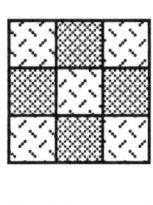

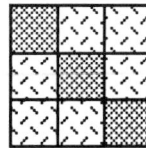

# PATCHWORK SHAPES AND BLOCK DESIGNS

## SPLIT NINE-PATCH

- 24 cm block (3 x 3 squares, each 8 cm)
  Cut square A 9.5 cm square
  Cut half-square triangle B from 10.5 cm square
- 30 cm block (3 x 3 squares, each 10 cm)
  Cut square A 11.5 cm square
  Cut half-square triangle B from 12.5 cm square

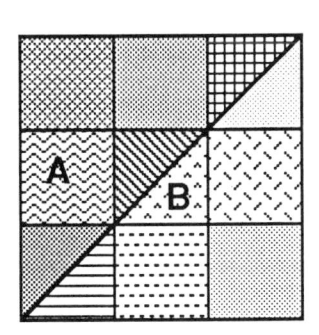

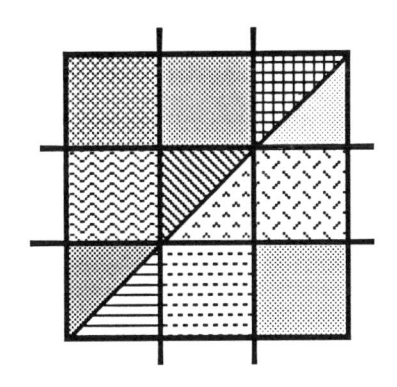

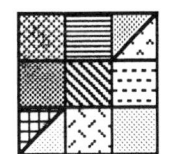

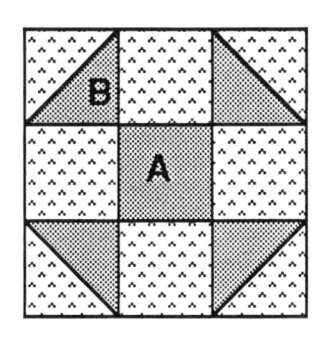

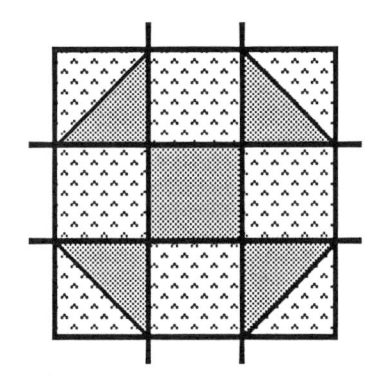

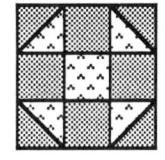

## SHOO-FLY

- 24 cm block (3 x 3 squares, each 8 cm)
  Cut square A 9.5 cm square
  Cut half-square triangle B from 10.5 cm square
- 30 cm block (3 x 3 squares, each 10 cm)
  Cut square A 11.5 cm square
  Cut half-square triangle B from 12.5 cm square

## DOUBLE X (9-PATCH)

- 24 cm block (3 x 3 squares, each 8 cm)
  Cut square A 9.5 cm square
  Cut half-square triangle B from 10.5 cm square
- 30 cm block (3 x 3 squares, each 10 cm)
  Cut square A 11.5 cm square
  Cut half-square triangle B from 12.5 cm square

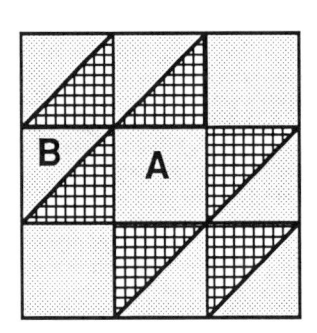

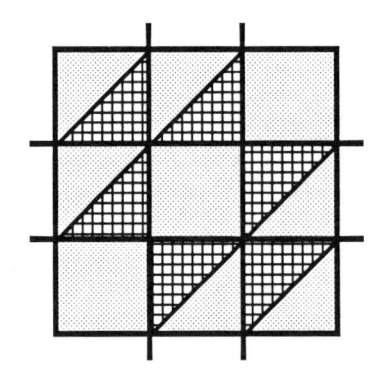

## MILKY WAY

- 24 cm block (3 x 3 squares, each 8 cm)
  Cut square A 9.5 cm square
  Cut half-square triangle B from 10.5 cm square
  Cut square C 5.5 cm square
- 30 cm block (3 x 3 squares, each 10 cm)
  Cut square A 11.5 cm square
  Cut half-square triangle B from 12.5 cm square
  Cut square C 6.5 cm square

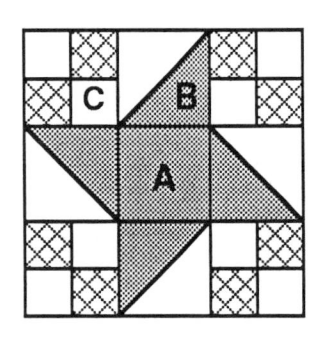

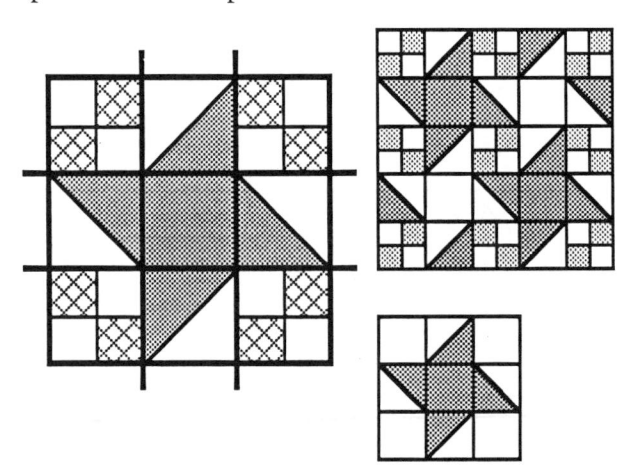

## BIRDS IN THE AIR (9-PATCH)

- 18 cm block (3 x 3 squares, each 6 cm)
  Cut half-square triangle A from 20.5 cm square
  Cut half-square triangle B from 8.5 cm square
- 24 cm block (3 x 3 squares, each 8 cm)
  Cut half-square triangle A from 26.5 cm square
  Cut half-square triangle B from 10.5 cm square

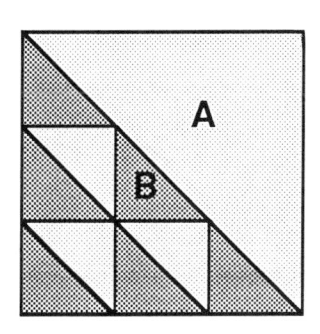

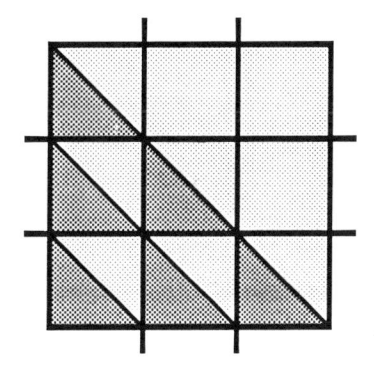

## CHURN DASH

- 18 cm block (3 x 3 squares, each 6 cm)
  Cut square A 7.5 cm square
  Cut half-square triangle B from 8.5 cm square
  Cut rectangle C 4.5 cm x 7.5 cm
- 24 cm block (3 x 3 squares, each 8 cm)
  Cut square A 9.5 cm square
  Cut half-square triangle B from 10.5 cm square
  Cut rectangle C 5.5 cm x 9.5 cm
- 30 cm block (3 x 3 squares, each 10 cm)
  Cut square A 11.5 cm square
  Cut half-square triangle B from 12.5 cm square
  Cut rectangle C 6.5 cm x 11.5 cm

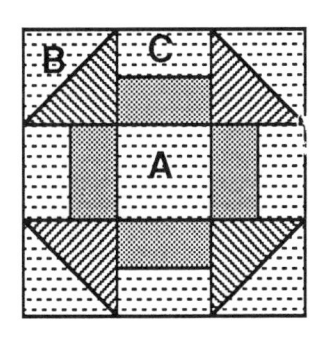

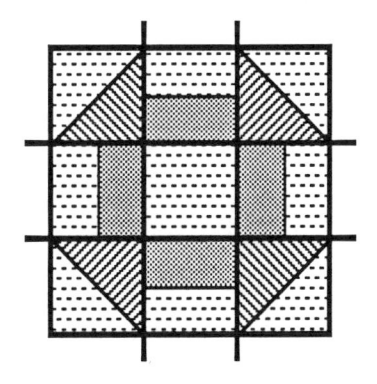

## OHIO STAR

- 24 cm block (3 x 3 squares, each 8 cm)
  Cut square A 9.5 cm square
  Cut quarter-square triangle B from 11.5 cm square
- 30 cm block (3 x 3 squares, each 10 cm)
  Cut square A 11.5 cm square
  Cut quarter-square triangle B from 13.5 cm square

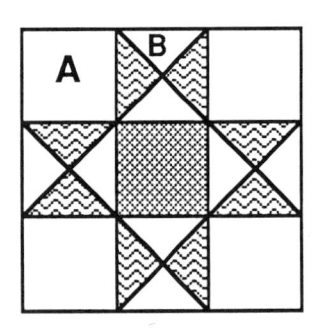

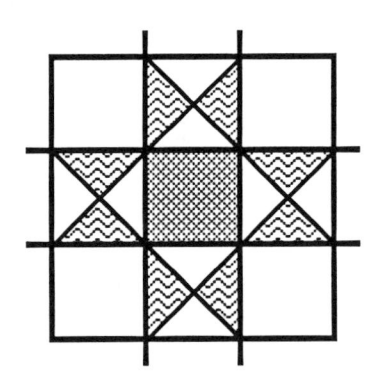

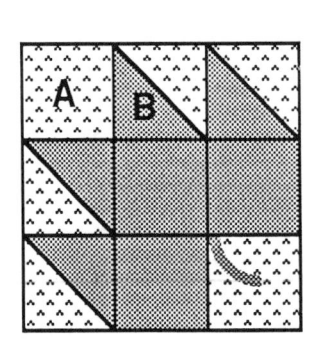

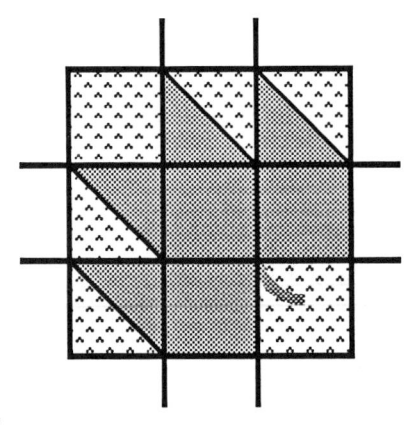

## MAPLE LEAF

(Stem of leaf is appliquéd — see p. 42)

- 18 cm block (3 x 3 squares, each 6 cm)
  Cut square A 7.5 cm square
  Cut half-square triangle B from 8.5 cm square
- 24 cm block (3 x 3 squares, each 8 cm)
  Cut square A 9.5 cm square
  Cut half-square triangle B from 10.5 cm square
- 30 cm block (3 x 3 squares, each 10 cm)
  Cut square A 11.5 cm square
  Cut half-square triangle B from 12.5 cm square

# PATCHWORK SHAPES AND BLOCK DESIGNS

BASKET

(Basket handle is appliquéd — see p. 42)
- 18 cm block (3 x 3 squares, each 6 cm)
  Cut half-square triangle A from 14.5 cm square
  Cut square B 7.5 cm square
  Cut half-square triangle C from 8.5 cm square
- 24 cm block (3 x 3 squares, each 8 cm)
  Cut half-square triangle A from 18.5 cm square
  Cut square B 9.5 cm square
  Cut half-square triangle C from 10.5 cm square

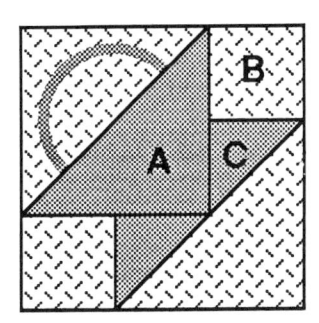

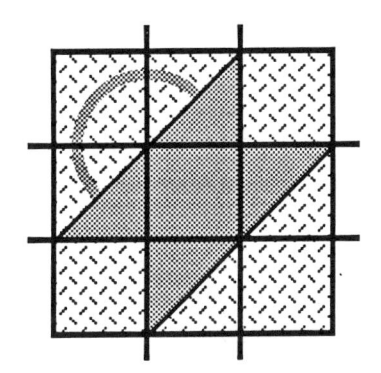

JACOB'S LADDER

- 24 cm block (3 x 3 squares, each 8 cm)
  Cut half-square triangle A from 10.5 cm square
  Cut square B 5.5 cm square
- 30 cm block (3 x 3 squares, each 10 cm)
  Cut half-square triangle A from 12.5 cm square
  Cut square B 6.5 cm square

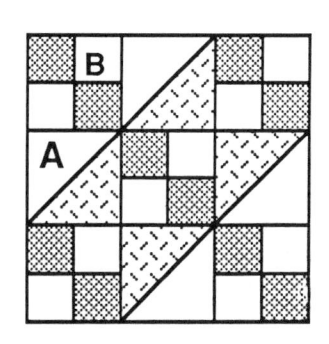

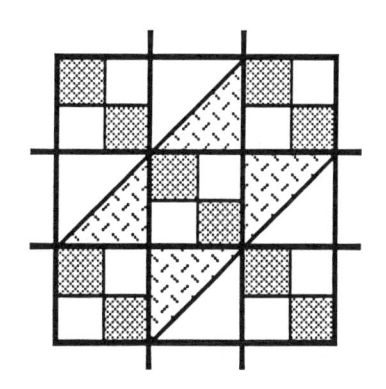

# METRIC QUILTMAKING

### 4-PATCH — 4 x 4 SQUARES

4-patch blocks can have a grid of 4 x 4 squares imposed on them. Choose block sizes which are multiples of four, such as 16 cm, 24 cm, 32 cm and 36 cm.

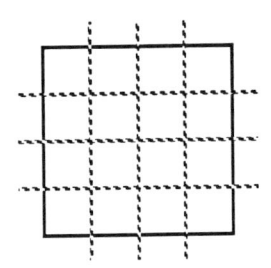

## FOUR-PATCH

- 12 cm block (4 x 4 squares, each 3 cm)
  Cut square A 7.5 cm square
- 16 cm block (4 x 4 squares, each 4 cm)
  Cut square A 9.5 cm square
- 20 cm block (4 x 4 squares, each 5 cm)
  Cut square A 11.5 cm square
- 24 cm block (4 x 4 squares, each 6 cm)
  Cut square A 13.5 cm square

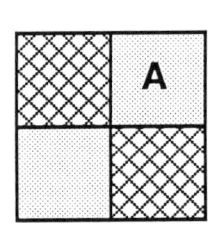

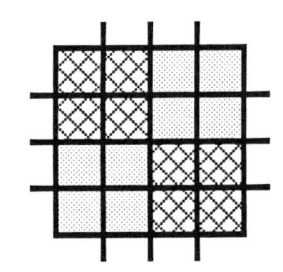

## PINWHEEL

- 12 cm block (4 x 4 squares, each 3 cm)
  Cut half-square triangle A from 8.5 cm square
- 16 cm block (4 x 4 squares, each 4 cm)
  Cut half-square triangle A from 10.5 cm square
- 20 cm block (4 x 4 squares, each 5 cm)
  Cut half-square triangle A from 12.5 cm square
- 24 cm block (4 x 4 squares, each 6 cm)
  Cut half-square triangle A from 14.5 cm square

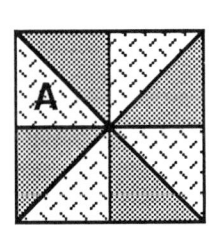

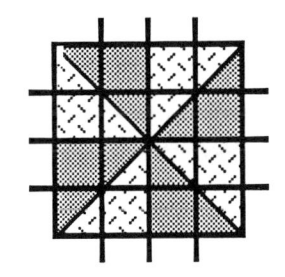

# PATCHWORK SHAPES AND BLOCK DESIGNS

## YANKEE PUZZLE

- 20 cm block (4 x 4 squares, each 5 cm)
  Cut quarter-square triangle A from 13.5 cm square
- 24 cm block (4 x 4 squares, each 6 cm)
  Cut quarter-square triangle A from 15.5 cm square
- 32 cm block (4 x 4 squares, each 8 cm)
  Cut quarter-square triangle A from 19.5 cm square

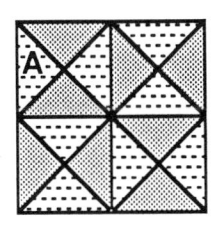

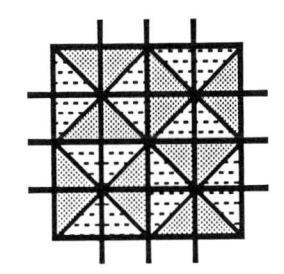

## WHIRLIGIG

- 20 cm block (4 x 4 squares, each 5 cm)
  Cut half-square triangle A from 12.5 cm square
  Cut quarter-square triangle B from 13.5 cm square
- 24 cm block (4 x 4 squares, each 6 cm)
  Cut half-square triangle A from 14.5 cm square
  Cut quarter-square triangle B from 15.5 cm square
- 32 cm block (4 x 4 squares, each 8 cm)
  Cut half-square triangle A from 18.5 cm square
  Cut quarter-square triangle B from 19.5 cm square

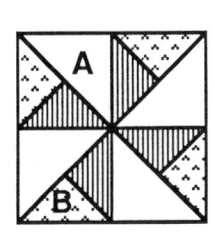

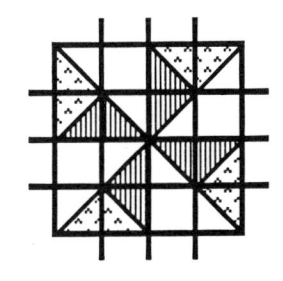

## METRIC QUILTMAKING

### BUCKEYE BEAUTY

- 20 cm block (4 x 4 squares, each 5 cm)
  Cut half-square triangle A from 12.5 cm square
  Cut square B 6.5 cm square
- 24 cm block (4 x 4 squares, each 6 cm)
  Cut half-square triangle A from 14.5 cm square
  Cut square B 7.5 cm square
- 32 cm block (4 x 4 squares, each 8 cm)
  Cut half-square triangle A from 18.5 cm square
  Cut square B 9.5 cm square

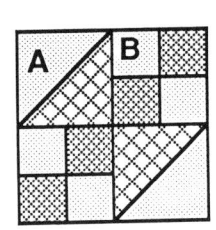

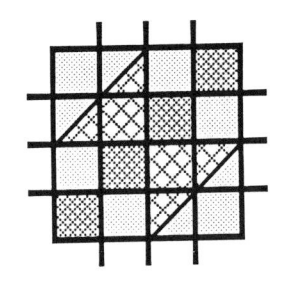

### SAWTOOTH STAR

- 20 cm block (4 x 4 squares, each 5 cm)
  Cut square A 6.5 cm square
  Cut half-square triangle B from 7.5 cm square
  Cut square C 11.5 cm square
- 24 cm block (4 x 4 squares, each 6 cm)
  Cut square A 7.5 cm square
  Cut half-square triangle B from 8.5 cm square
  Cut square C 13.5 cm square
- 32 cm block (4 x 4 squares, each 8 cm)
  Cut square A 9.5 cm square
  Cut half-square triangle B from 10.5 cm square
  Cut square C 17.5 cm square

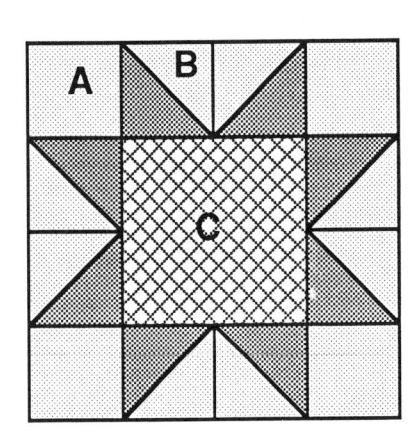

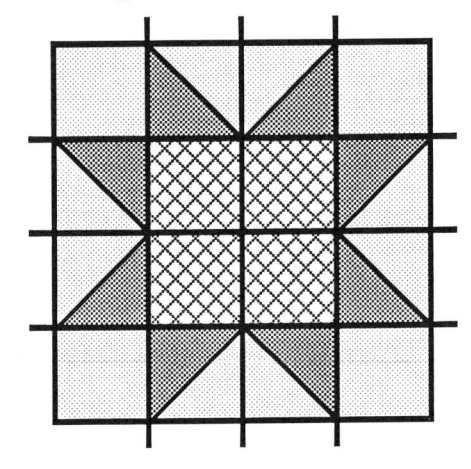

# PATCHWORK SHAPES AND BLOCK DESIGNS

## INDIAN STAR

- 20 cm block (4 x 4 squares, each 5 cm)
  Cut square A 6.5 cm square
  Cut half-square triangle B from 7.5 cm square
- 24 cm block (4 x 4 squares, each 6 cm)
  Cut square A 7.5 cm square
  Cut half-square triangle B from 8.5 cm square
- 32 cm block (4 x 4 squares, each 8 cm)
  Cut square A 9.5 cm square
  Cut half-square triangle B from 10.5 cm square

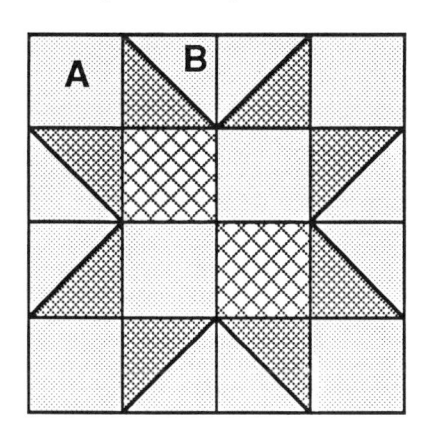

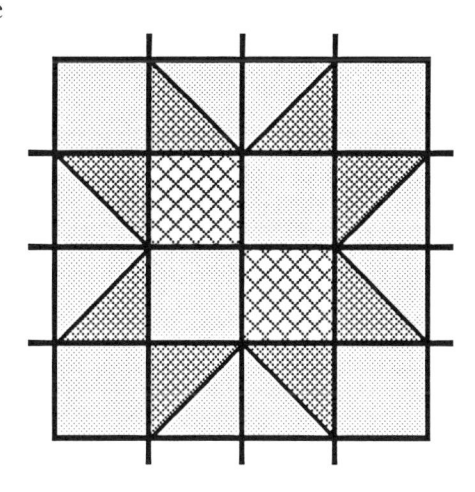

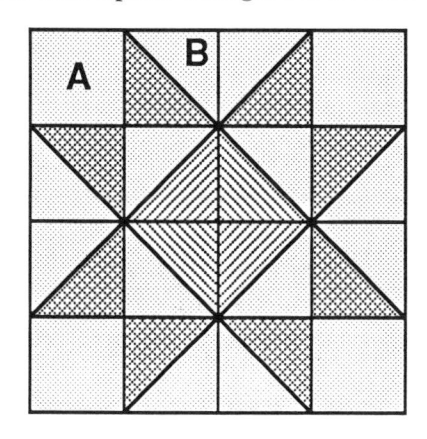

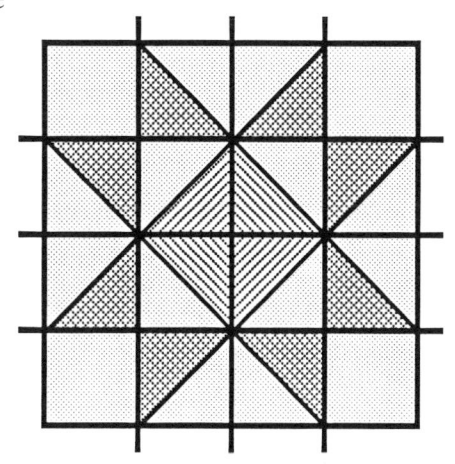

## EVENING STAR

- 20 cm block (4 x 4 squares, each 5 cm)
  Cut square A 6.5 cm square
  Cut half-square triangle B from 7.5 cm square
- 24 cm block (4 x 4 squares, each 6 cm)
  Cut square A 7.5 cm square
  Cut half-square triangle B from 8.5 cm square
- 32 cm block (4 x 4 squares, each 8 cm)
  Cut square A 9.5 cm square
  Cut half-square triangle B from 10.5 cm square

# METRIC QUILTMAKING

## ROAD TO OKLAHOMA

- 20 cm block (4 x 4 squares, each 5 cm)
  Cut square A 6.5 cm square
  Cut half-square triangle B from 7.5 cm square
- 24 cm block (4 x 4 squares, each 6 cm)
  Cut square A 7.5 cm square
  Cut half-square triangle B from 8.5 cm square
- 32 cm block (4 x 4 squares, each 8 cm)
  Cut square A 9.5 cm square
  Cut half-square triangle B from 10.5 cm square

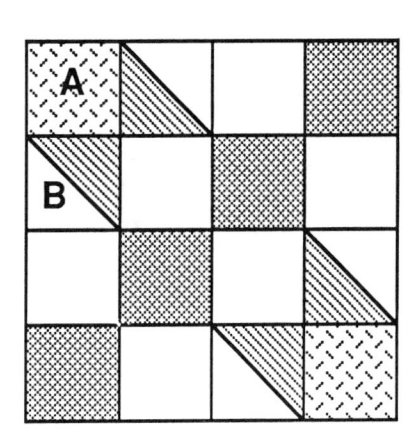

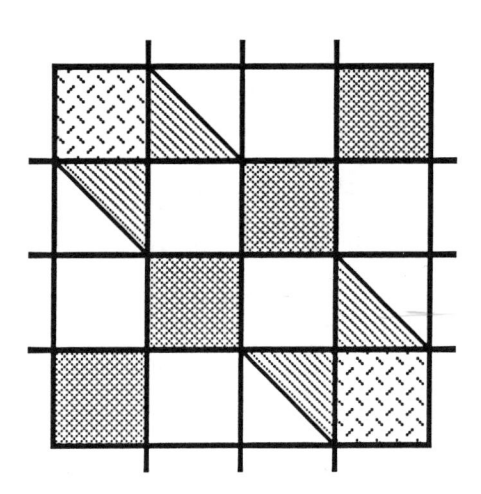

## OLD MAID'S PUZZLE

- 20 cm block (4 x 4 squares, each 5 cm)
  Cut half-square triangle A from 12.5 cm square
  Cut square B 6.5 cm square
  Cut half-square triangle C from 7.5 cm square
- 24 cm block (4 x 4 squares, each 6 cm)
  Cut half-square triangle A from 14.5 cm square
  Cut square B 7.5 cm square
  Cut half-square triangle C from 8.5 cm square
- 32 cm block (4 x 4 squares, each 8 cm)
  Cut half-square triangle A from 18.5 cm square
  Cut square B 9.5 cm square
  Cut half-square triangle C from 10.5 cm square

# PATCHWORK SHAPES AND BLOCK DESIGNS

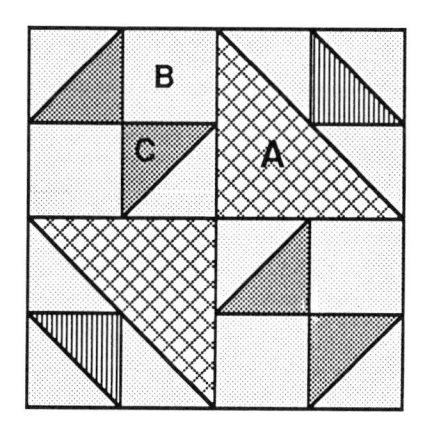

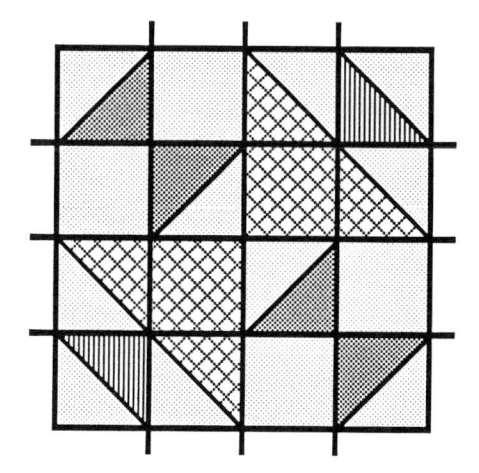

## DUTCHMAN'S PUZZLE

- 20 cm block (4 x 4 squares, each 5 cm)
  Cut half-square triangle A from 7.5 cm square
  Cut quarter-square triangle B from 13.5 cm square
- 24 cm block (4 x 4 squares, each 6 cm)
  Cut half-square triangle A from 8.5 cm square
  Cut quarter-square triangle B from 15.5 cm square
- 32 cm block (4 x 4 squares, each 8 cm)
  Cut half-square triangle A from 10.5 cm square
  Cut quarter-square triangle B from 19.5 cm square

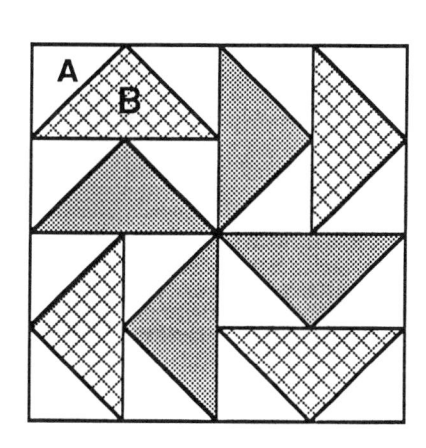

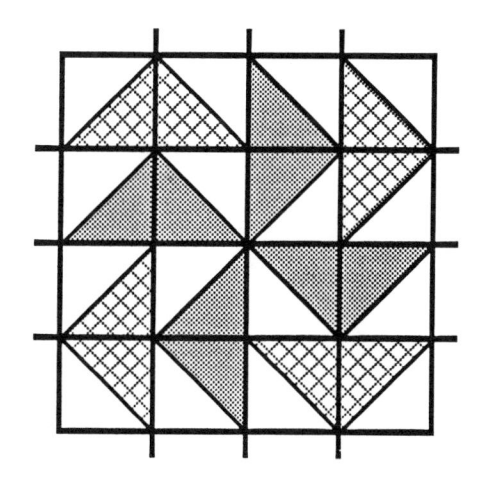

## FLOWER BASKET

- 20 cm block (4 x 4 squares, each 5 cm)
  Cut half-square triangle A from 7.5 cm square
  Cut half-square triangle B from 12.5 cm square
  Cut rectangle C 6.5 cm x 11.5 cm
- 24 cm block (4 x 4 squares, each 6 cm)
  Cut half-square triangle A from 8.5 cm square
  Cut half-square triangle B from 14.5 cm square
  Cut rectangle C 7.5 cm x 13.5 cm
- 32 cm block (4 x 4 squares, each 8 cm)
  Cut half-square triangle A from 10.5 cm square
  Cut half-square triangle B from 18.5 cm square
  Cut rectangle C 9.5 cm x 17.5 cm

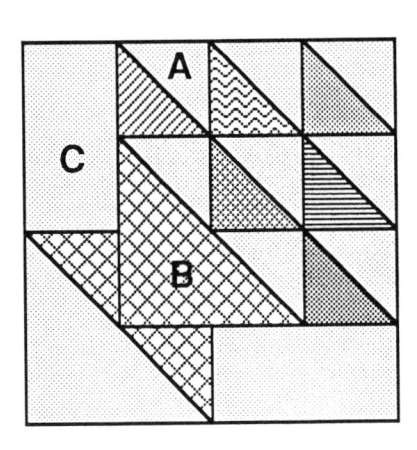

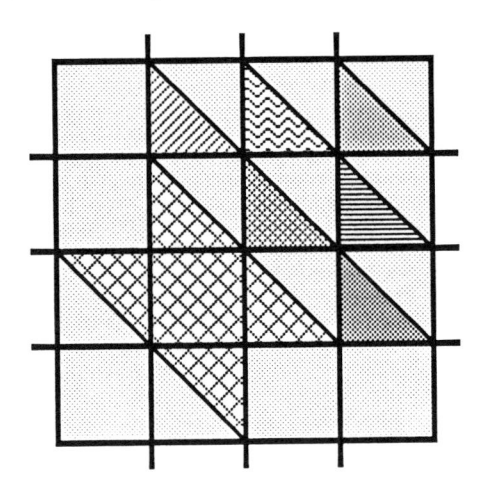

## KANSAS TROUBLES

- 32 cm block (4 x 4 squares, each 8 cm)
  Cut half-square triangle A from 18.5 cm square
  Cut half-square triangle B from 10.5 cm square
  Cut square C 5.5 cm square
  Cut half-square triangle D from 6.5 cm square
- 40 cm block (4 x 4 squares, each 10 cm)
  Cut half-square triangle A from 22.5 cm square
  Cut half-square triangle B from 12.5 cm square
  Cut square C 6.5 cm square
  Cut half-square triangle D from 7.5 cm square

# PATCHWORK SHAPES AND BLOCK DESIGNS

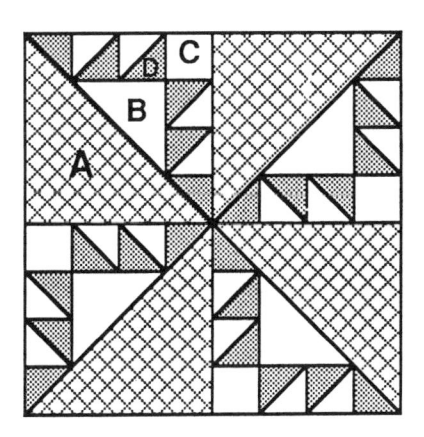

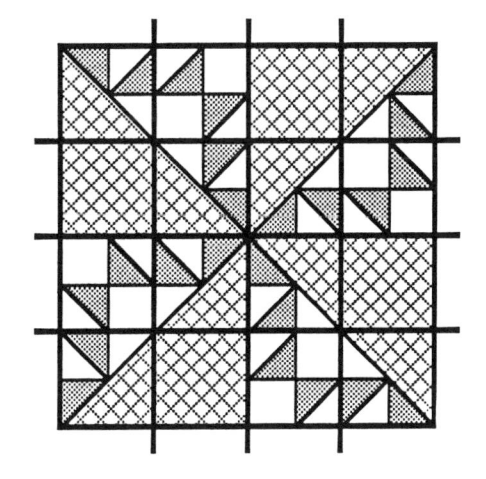

ANVIL

- 24 cm block (4 x 4 squares, each 6 cm)
  Cut square A 7.5 cm square
  Cut half-square triangle B from 14.5 cm square
  Cut half-square triangle C from 8.5 cm square
  Cut square D 13.5 cm square
- 32 cm block (4 x 4 squares, each 8 cm)
  Cut square A 9.5 cm square
  Cut half-square triangle B from 18.5 cm square
  Cut half-square triangle C from 10.5 cm square
  Cut square D 17.5 cm square

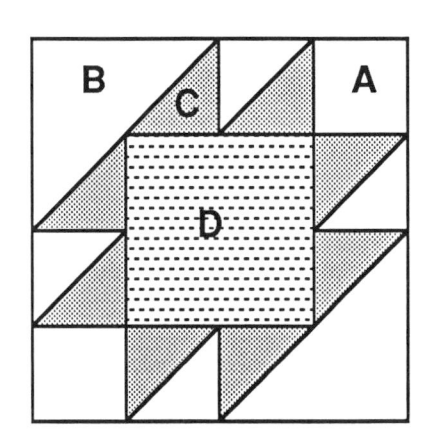

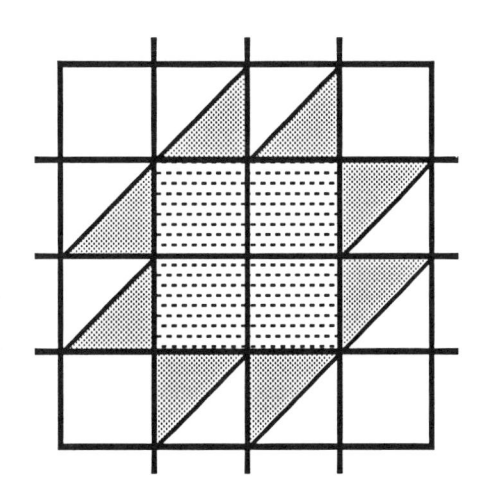

## PUSS IN THE CORNER

(This block is sometimes called Nine-patch because it is made up of nine pieces, but, in fact, it is a 4-patch block.)

- 20 cm block (4 x 4 squares, each 5 cm)
  Cut square A 6.5 cm square
  Cut square B 11.5 cm square
  Cut rectangle C 6.5 cm x 11.5 cm
- 24 cm block (4 x 4 squares, each 6 cm)
  Cut square A 7.5 cm square
  Cut square B 13.5 cm square
  Cut rectangle C 7.5 cm x 13.5 cm
- 32 cm block (4 x 4 squares, each 8 cm)
  Cut square A 9.5 cm square
  Cut square B 17.5 cm square
  Cut rectangle C 9.5 cm x 17.5 cm

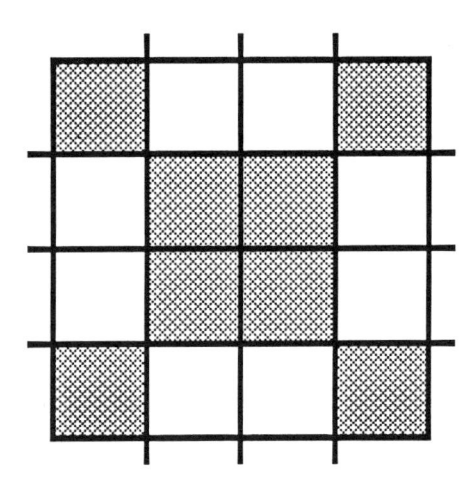

## OCEAN WAVES

- 32 cm block (4 x 4 squares, each 8 cm)
  Cut quarter-square triangle A from 11.5 cm square
  Cut square B 17.5 cm square
- 40 cm block (4 x 4 squares, each 10 cm)
  Cut quarter-square triangle A from 13.5 cm square
  Cut square B 21.5 cm square

# PATCHWORK SHAPES AND BLOCK DESIGNS

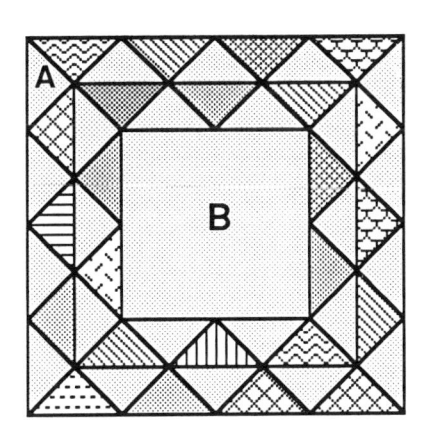

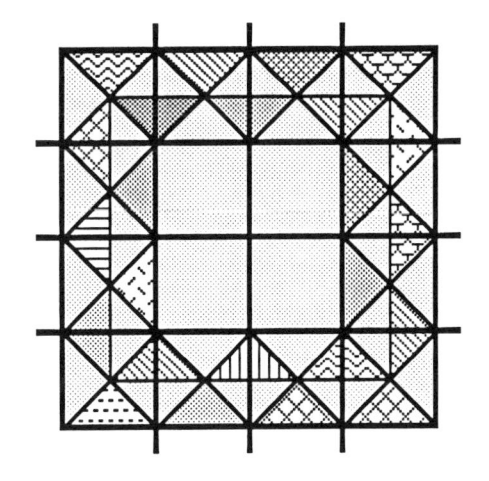

SAILING SHIP

- 20 cm block (4 x 4 squares, each 5 cm)
  Cut half-square triangle A from 7.5 cm square
  Cut rectangle B 6.5 cm x 11.5 cm
  Cut rectangle C 6.5 cm x 21.5 cm
- 24 cm block (4 x 4 squares, each 6 cm)
  Cut half-square triangle A from 8.5 cm square
  Cut rectangle B 7.5 cm x 13.5 cm
  Cut rectangle C 7.5 cm x 25.5 cm
- 32 cm block (4 x 4 squares, each 8 cm)
  Cut half-square triangle A from 10.5 cm square
  Cut rectangle B 9.5 cm x 17.5 cm
  Cut rectangle C 9.5 cm x 33.5 cm

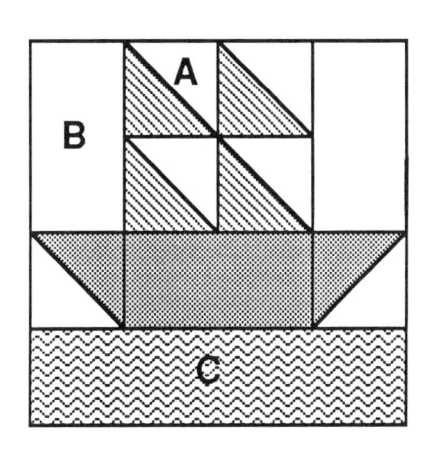

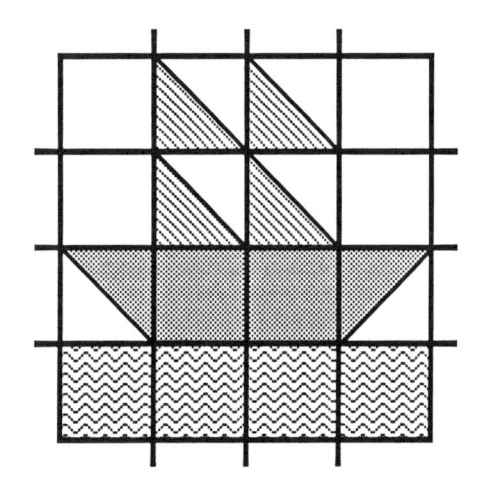

## MOSAIC

- 20 cm block (4 x 4 squares, each 5 cm)
  Cut half-square triangle A from 7.5 cm square
- 24 cm block (4 x 4 squares, each 6 cm)
  Cut half-square triangle A from 8.5 cm square
- 32 cm block (4 x 4 squares, each 8 cm)
  Cut half-square triangle A from 10.5 cm square

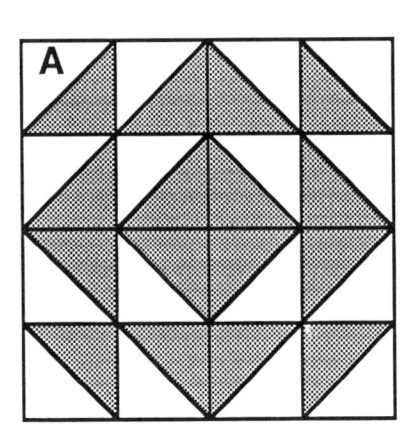

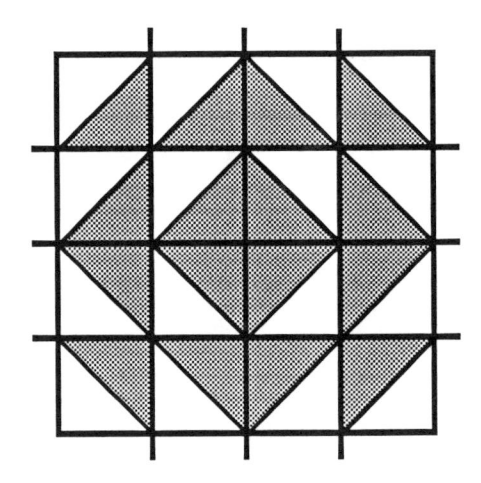

## BIRDS IN THE AIR (4-PATCH)

- 20 cm block (4 x 4 squares, each 5 cm)
  Cut half-square triangle A from 7.5 cm square
  Cut half-square triangle B from 12.5 cm square
- 24 cm block (4 x 4 squares, each 6 cm)
  Cut half-square triangle A from 8.5 cm square
  Cut half-square triangle B from 14.5 cm square
- 32 cm block (4 x 4 squares, each 8 cm)
  Cut half-square triangle A from 10.5 cm square
  Cut half-square triangle B from 18.5 cm square

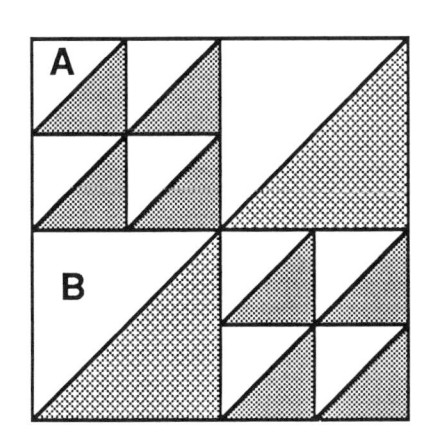

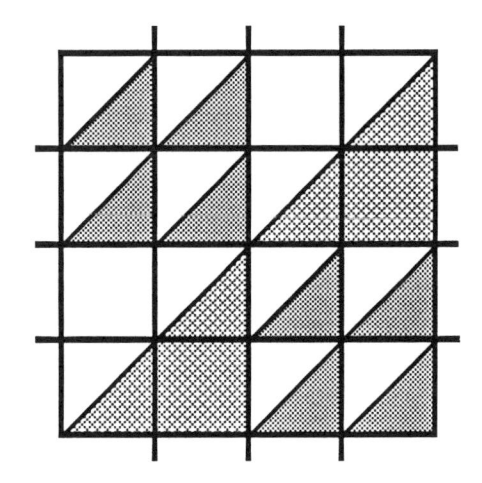

## DOUBLE X (4-PATCH)

- 20 cm block (4 x 4 squares, each 5 cm)
  Cut square A 6.5 cm square
  Cut half-square triangle B from 7.5 cm square
  Cut half-square triangle C from 12.5 cm square
- 24 cm block (4 x 4 squares, each 6 cm)
  Cut square A 7.5 cm square
  Cut half-square triangle B from 8.5 cm square
  Cut half-square triangle C from 14.5 cm square
- 32 cm block (4 x 4 squares, each 8 cm)
  Cut square A 9.5 cm square
  Cut half-square triangle B from 10.5 cm square
  Cut half-square triangle C from 18.5 cm square

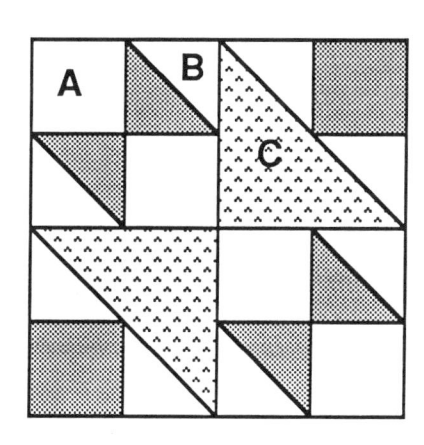

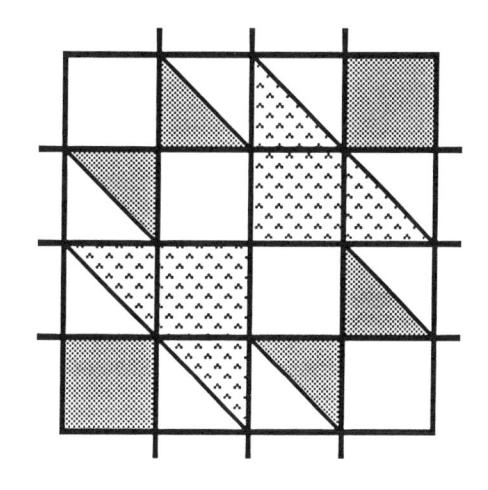

## DIAMOND STAR

- 20 cm block (4 x 4 squares, each 5 cm)
  Cut square A 6.5 cm square
  Cut half-square triangle B from 7.5 cm square
- 24 cm block (4 x 4 squares, each 6 cm)
  Cut square A 7.5 cm square
  Cut half-square triangle B from 8.5 cm square
- 32 cm block (4 x 4 squares, each 8 cm)
  Cut square A 9.5 cm square
  Cut half-square triangle B from 10.5 cm square

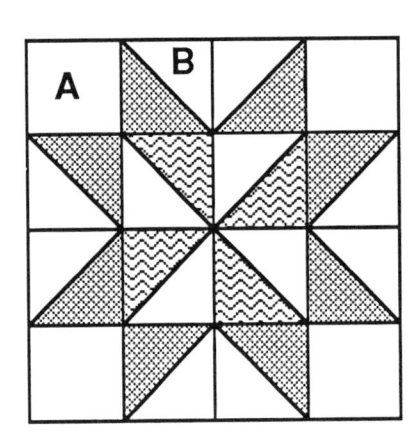

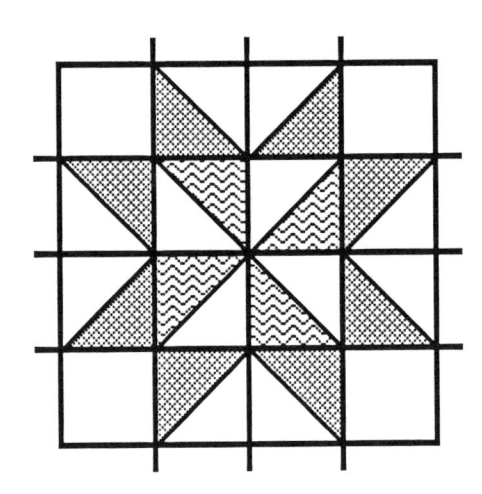

### 5-PATCH — 5 X 5 SQUARES

5-patch blocks are those which can have a grid of 5 x 5 squares imposed on them. Choose block sizes which are multiples of five, such as 20 cm, 25 cm and 30 cm.

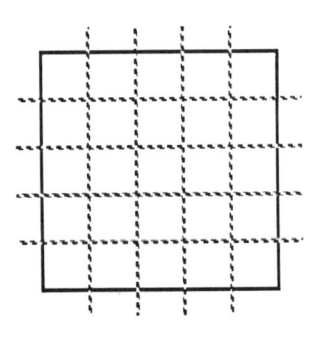

# PATCHWORK SHAPES AND BLOCK DESIGNS

## DOUBLE WRENCH

- 25 cm block (5 x 5 squares, each 5 cm)
  Cut half-square triangle A from 12.5 cm square
  Cut square B 6.5 cm square
- 30 cm block (5 x 5 squares, each 6 cm)
  Cut half-square triangle A from 14.5 cm square
  Cut square B 7.5 cm square

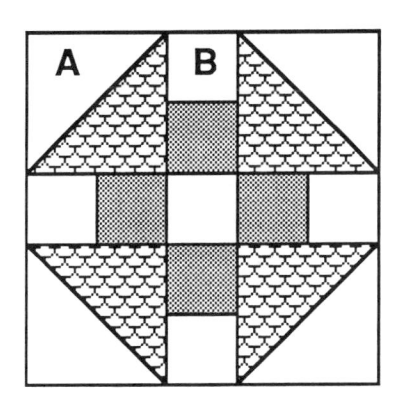

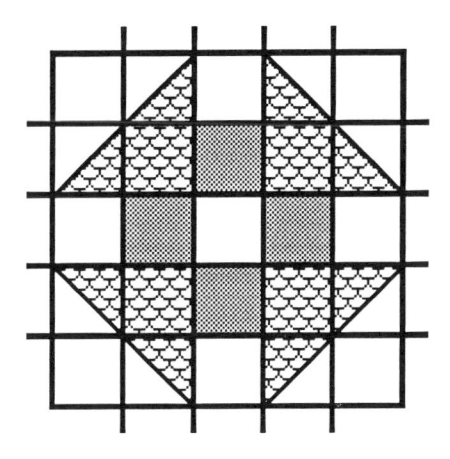

## DUCK AND DUCKLINGS

- 25 cm block (5 x 5 squares, each 5 cm)
  Cut half-square triangle A from 7.5 cm square
  Cut half-square triangle B from 12.5 cm square
  Cut square C 6.5 cm square
  Cut rectangle D 6.5 cm x 11.5 cm
- 30 cm block (5 x 5 squares, each 6 cm)
  Cut half-square triangle A from 8.5 cm square
  Cut half-square triangle B from 14.5 cm square
  Cut square C 7.5 cm square
  Cut rectangle D 7.5 cm x 13.5 cm

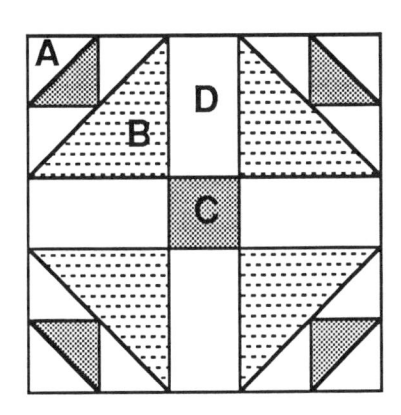

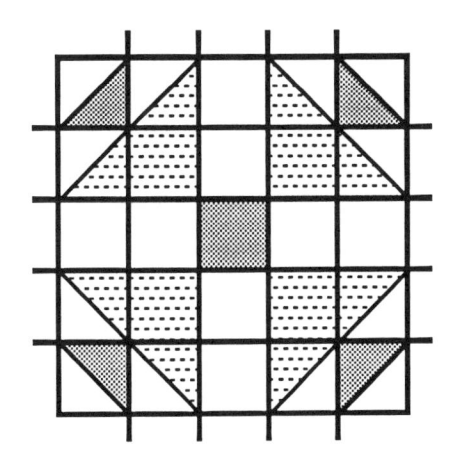

# METRIC QUILTMAKING

## WEDDING RING

- 25 cm block (5 x 5 squares, each 5 cm)
  Cut half-square triangle A from 7.5 cm square
  Cut square B 6.5 cm square
- 30 cm block (5 x 5 squares, each 6 cm)
  Cut half-square triangle A from 8.5 cm square
  Cut square B 7.5 cm square

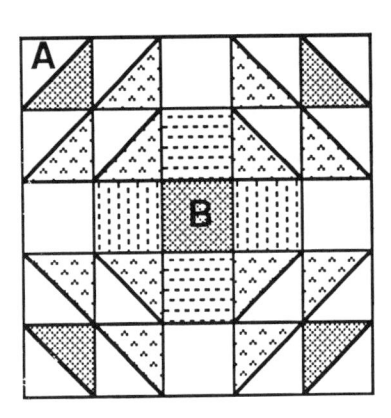

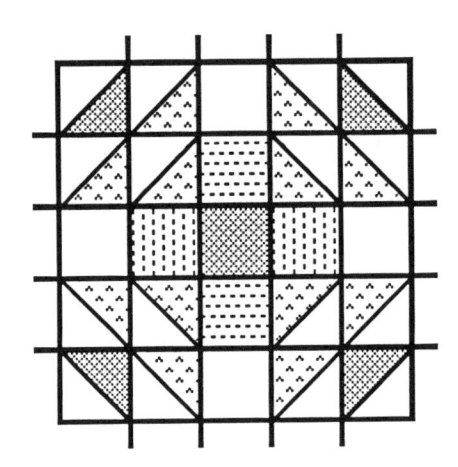

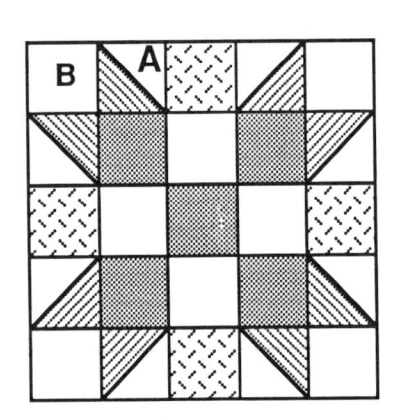

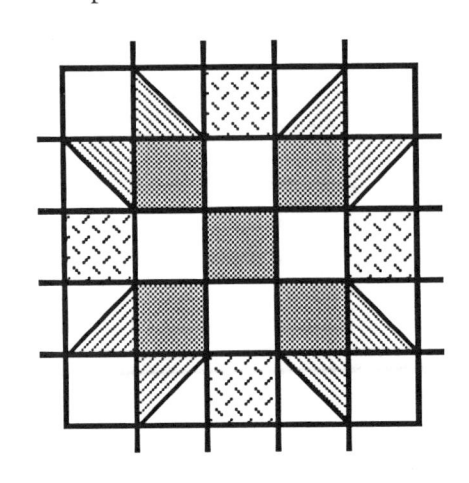

## FOUR X STAR

- 25 cm block (5 x 5 squares, each 5 cm)
  Cut half-square triangle A from 7.5 cm square
  Cut square B 6.5 cm square
- 30 cm block (5 x 5 squares, each 6 cm)
  Cut half-square triangle A from 8.5 cm square
  Cut square B 7.5 cm square

# PATCHWORK SHAPES AND BLOCK DESIGNS

## FLYING GEESE

- 25 cm block (5 x 5 squares, each 5 cm)
  Cut half-square triangle A from 7.5 cm square
  Cut square B 6.5 cm square
  Cut rectangle C 6.5 cm x 11.5 cm
- 30 cm block (5 x 5 squares, each 6 cm)
  Cut half-square triangle A from 8.5 cm square
  Cut square B 7.5 cm square
  Cut rectangle C 7.5 cm x 13.5 cm

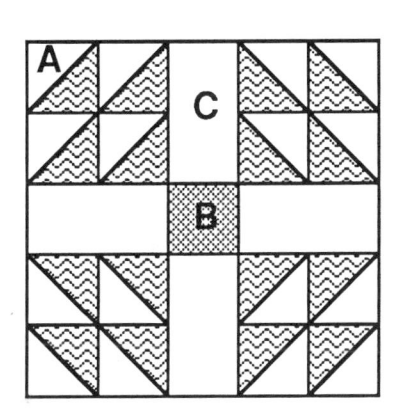

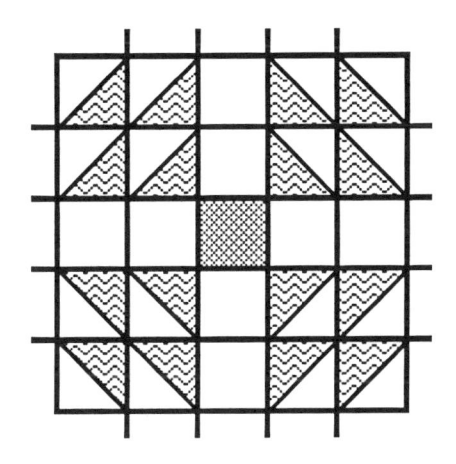

## LADY OF THE LAKE

- 25 cm block (5 x 5 squares, each 5 cm)
  Cut half-square triangle A from 7.5 cm square
  Cut half-square triangle B from 17.5 cm square
- 30 cm block (5 x 5 squares, each 6 cm)
  Cut half-square triangle A from 8.5 cm square
  Cut half-square triangle B from 20.5 cm square

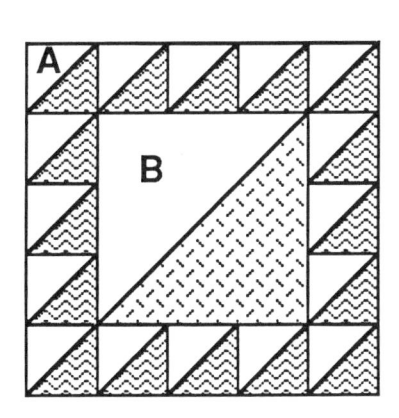

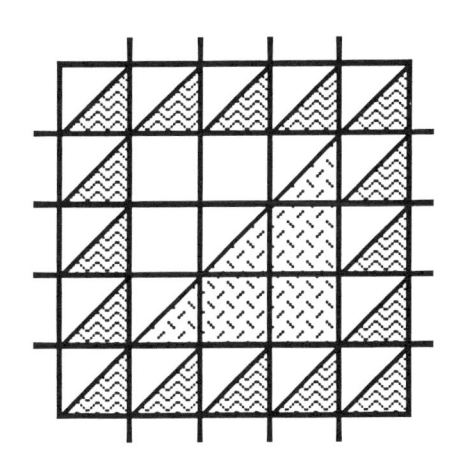

CAKE STAND

- 25 cm block (5 x 5 squares, each 5 cm)
  Cut square A 6.5 cm
  Cut half-square triangle B from 7.5 cm square
  Cut half-square triangle C from 17.5 cm square
  Cut half-square triangle D from 12.5 cm square
  Cut rectangle E 6.5 cm x 16.5 cm
- 30 cm block (5 x 5 squares, each 6 cm)
  Cut square A 7.5 cm
  Cut half-square triangle B from 8.5 cm square
  Cut half-square triangle C from 20.5 cm square
  Cut half-square triangle D from 14.5 cm square
  Cut rectangle E 7.5 cm x 19.5 cm

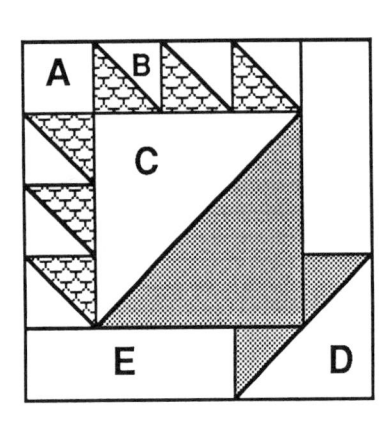

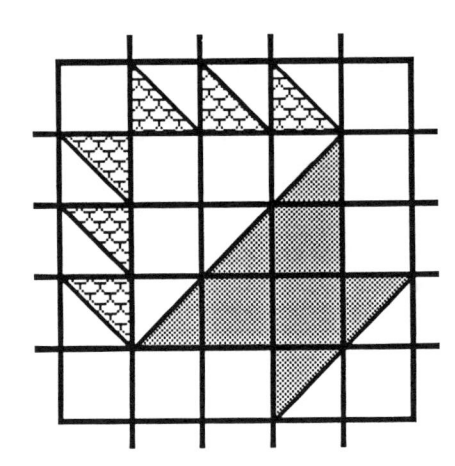

### 7-PATCH — 7 X 7 SQUARES

7-patch blocks are ones which can have a grid of 7 x 7 squares imposed on them. Choose block sizes which are multiples of seven, such as 28 cm and 35 cm.

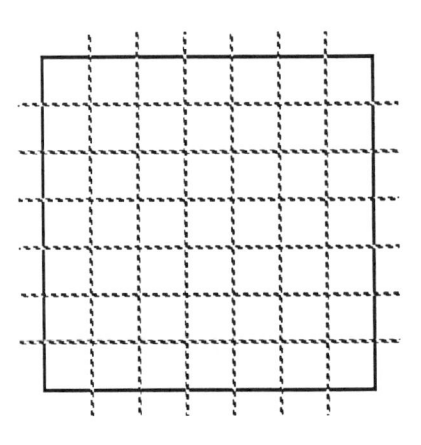

# PATCHWORK SHAPES AND BLOCK DESIGNS

## BEAR'S PAW

- 28 cm block (7 x 7 squares, each 4 cm)
  Cut square A 5.5 cm square
  Cut half-square triangle B from 6.5 cm square
  Cut square C 9.5 cm square
  Cut rectangle D 5.5 cm x 13.5 cm
- 35 cm block (7 x 7 squares, each 5 cm)
  Cut square A 6.5 cm square
  Cut half-square triangle B from 7.5 cm square
  Cut square C 11.5 cm square
  Cut rectangle D 6.5 cm x 16.5 cm

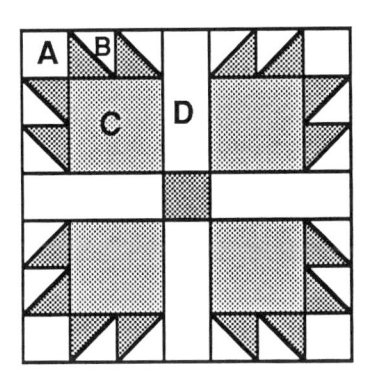

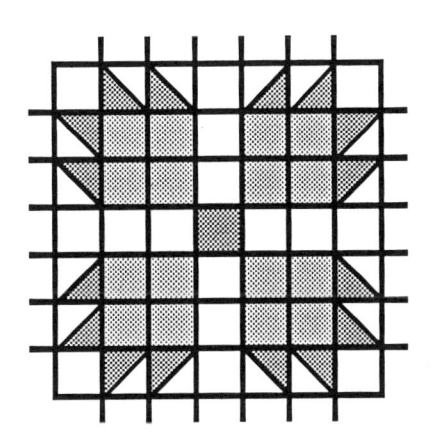

## HEN AND CHICKENS

- 28 cm block (7 x 7 squares, each 4 cm)
  Cut square A 5.5 cm square
  Cut half-square triangle B from 6.5 cm square
  Cut square C 9.5 cm square
  Cut rectangle D 5.5 cm x 13.5 cm
- 35 cm block (7 x 7 squares, each 5 cm)
  Cut square A 6.5 cm square
  Cut half-square triangle B from 7.5 cm square
  Cut square C 11.5 cm square
  Cut rectangle D 6.5 cm x 16.5 cm

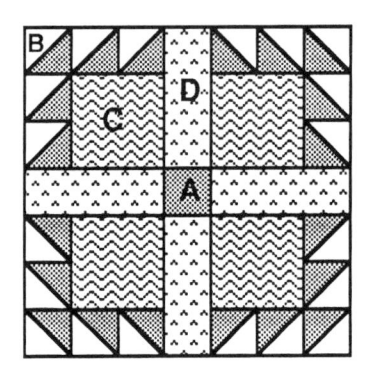

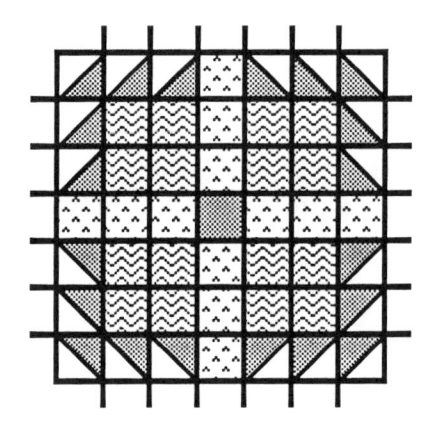

# METRIC QUILTMAKING

AUTUMN LEAVES

(Stems of leaves are appliquéd — see p. 42)

- 28 cm block (7 x 7 squares, each 4 cm)
  Cut square A 5.5 cm square
  Cut half-square triangle B from 6.5 cm square
  Cut rectangle C 5.5 cm x 13.5 cm

- 35 cm block (7 x 7 squares, each 5 cm)
  Cut square A 6.5 cm square
  Cut half-square triangle B from 7.5 cm square
  Cut rectangle C 6.5 cm x 16.5 cm square

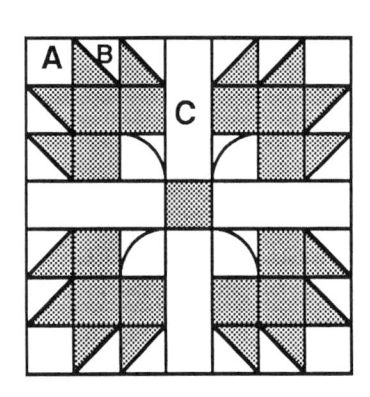

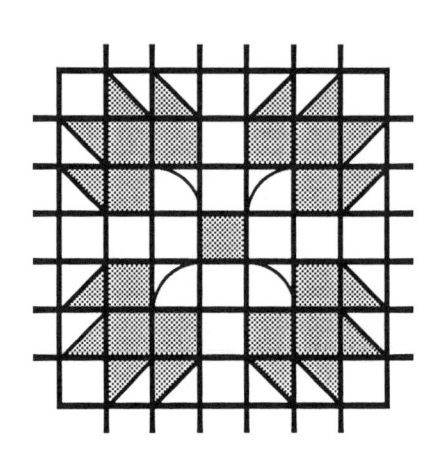

104

# SUMMER ROSES QUILT

Designed and made by Margaret Rolfe

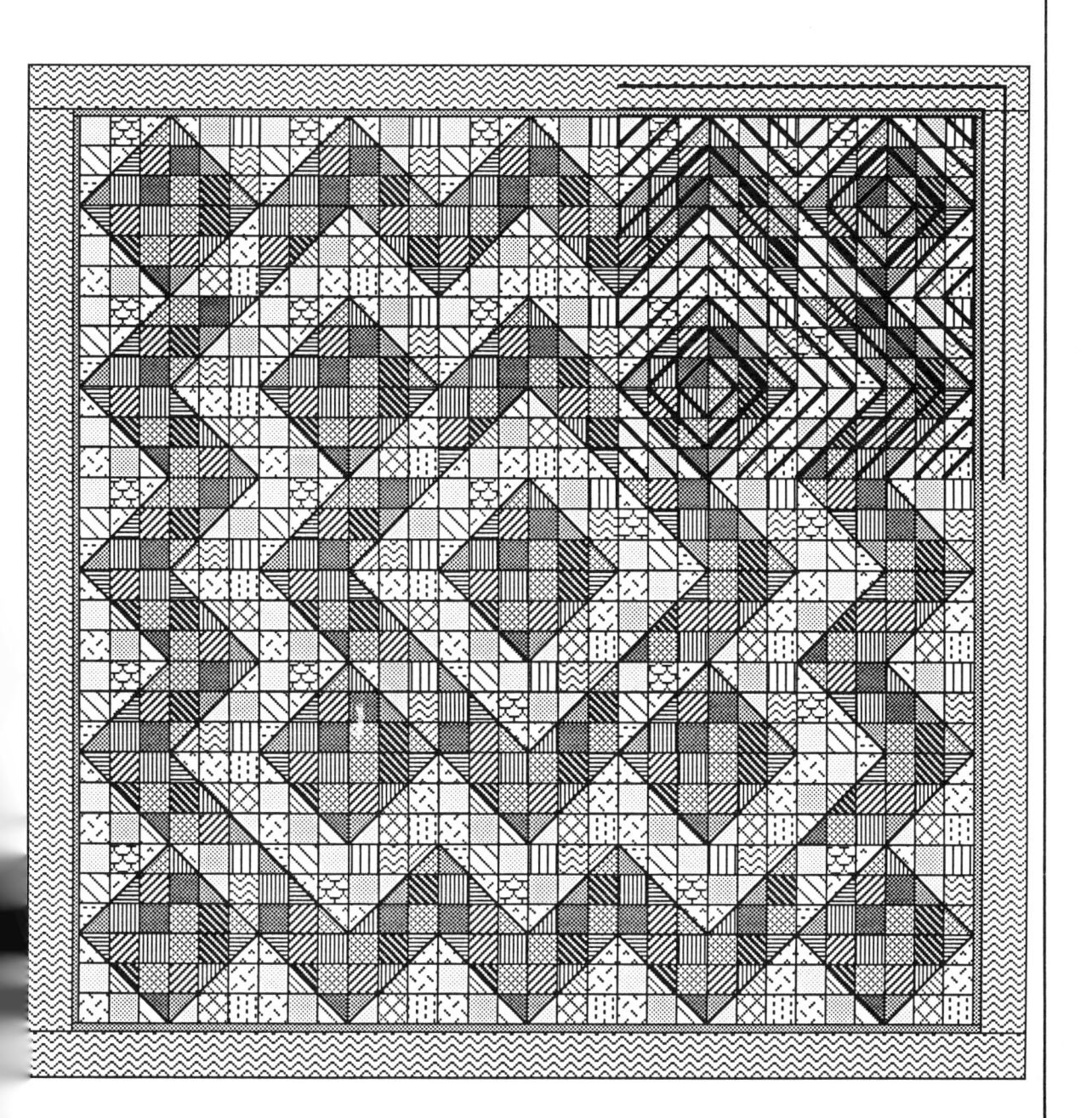

## METRIC QUILTMAKING

### QUILT INFORMATION (FINISHED SIZES)
Quilt top, 252 cm x 252 cm
100 Split Nine-patch blocks, each 22.5 cm x 22.5 cm, arranged in 10 x 10 rows
Inner border: 2 cm wide
Outer border: 11.5 cm wide

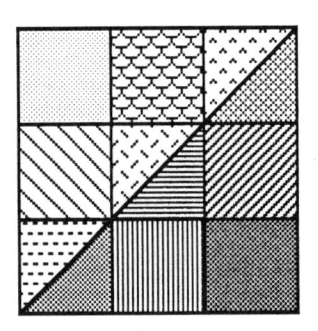

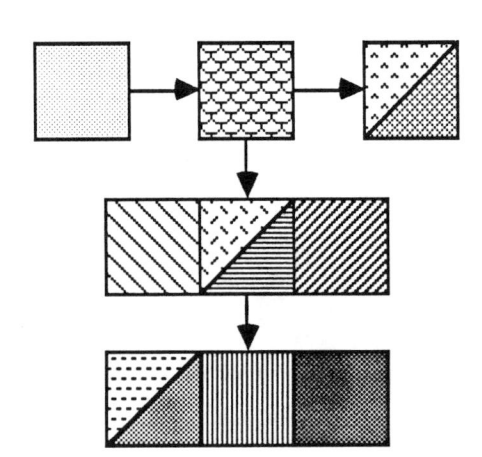

SPLIT NINE-PATCH BLOCK
Finished size of block, 22.5 cm x 22.5 cm
9-patch block, 3 x 3 squares, each 7.5 cm (finished size)


REQUIREMENTS (112 cm-wide fabric)
2.6 m blue print for Nine-patch blocks, outer border and binding
2.5 m total assorted light pink, light blue and cream prints for light side of Nine-patch blocks (include some variation of tonal values)
1.5 m total assorted blue and pink prints for the dark side of Nine-patch blocks (include some variation of tonal values)
1 m deep rose pink print for inner border and Nine-patch blocks
60 cm print with large pink roses on it (roses should be approximately 8–10 cm across)
262 cm x 262 cm batting
6.5 m backing fabric

# QUILT PROJECTS

## QUILT CONSTRUCTION

1. From blue border print, and cutting lengthways down the fabric, cut:
    Four strips, each 13 cm wide; set these strips aside for the outer border.
    Four strips, each 7 cm wide; set these strips aside for the binding.
    One strip, 9 cm wide; recut strip into 9 cm squares.
    One strip, 10 cm wide; recut strip into 10 cm squares, then re-cut the squares into half-square triangles.
2. From deep rose pink print, cut:
    Eight strips, each 3.5 cm wide; set these strips aside for the inner border.
    Three strips, each 9 cm wide; recut strip into 9 cm squares.
    Two strips, each 10 cm wide; recut strip into 10 cm squares, then recut the squares into half-square triangles.
3. From print with roses on it, cut five strips, each 9 cm wide; recut strips into 9 cm x 9 cm squares.
4. From both assortments of dark and light prints, cut approximately two thirds of each fabric into 9 cm x 9 cm squares; cut remaining third into 10 cm x 10 cm squares, and recut these squares into half-square triangles.

    In total, the quilt will require 300 light squares, 300 light half-square triangles, 300 dark squares and 300 dark half-square triangles. (Note that this total for the dark prints includes the squares and triangles which you have already cut out from the print with the roses on it, the deep rose print and the border print.)
5. Construct the Split Nine-patch blocks, balancing blue and pink and varying the tonal values within both light and dark sides of each block.
6. Pin up blocks as you complete them, to help you distribute the colours (especially the print with the roses on it) evenly around the quilt. The blocks should be arranged into 10 rows of 10 blocks each. Turn the blocks as required to make the pattern of lights and darks as shown in the quilt diagram. If space is limited to pin up the quilt, work each quarter of the quilt (five rows of five blocks) separately. Join blocks.
7. Following instructions for adding borders with squared corners, add inner border of deep rose print strips (strips will need to be joined to make lengths required), then add outer border of blue print strips.
8. Prepare backing fabric. Layer quilt top, batting and backing fabric, and tack (baste) together. Hand quilt (see p. 55), following the pattern indicated by thick (dark) lines on quilt diagram.
9. Bind quilt (see p. 60) with the already-cut strips of blue print.

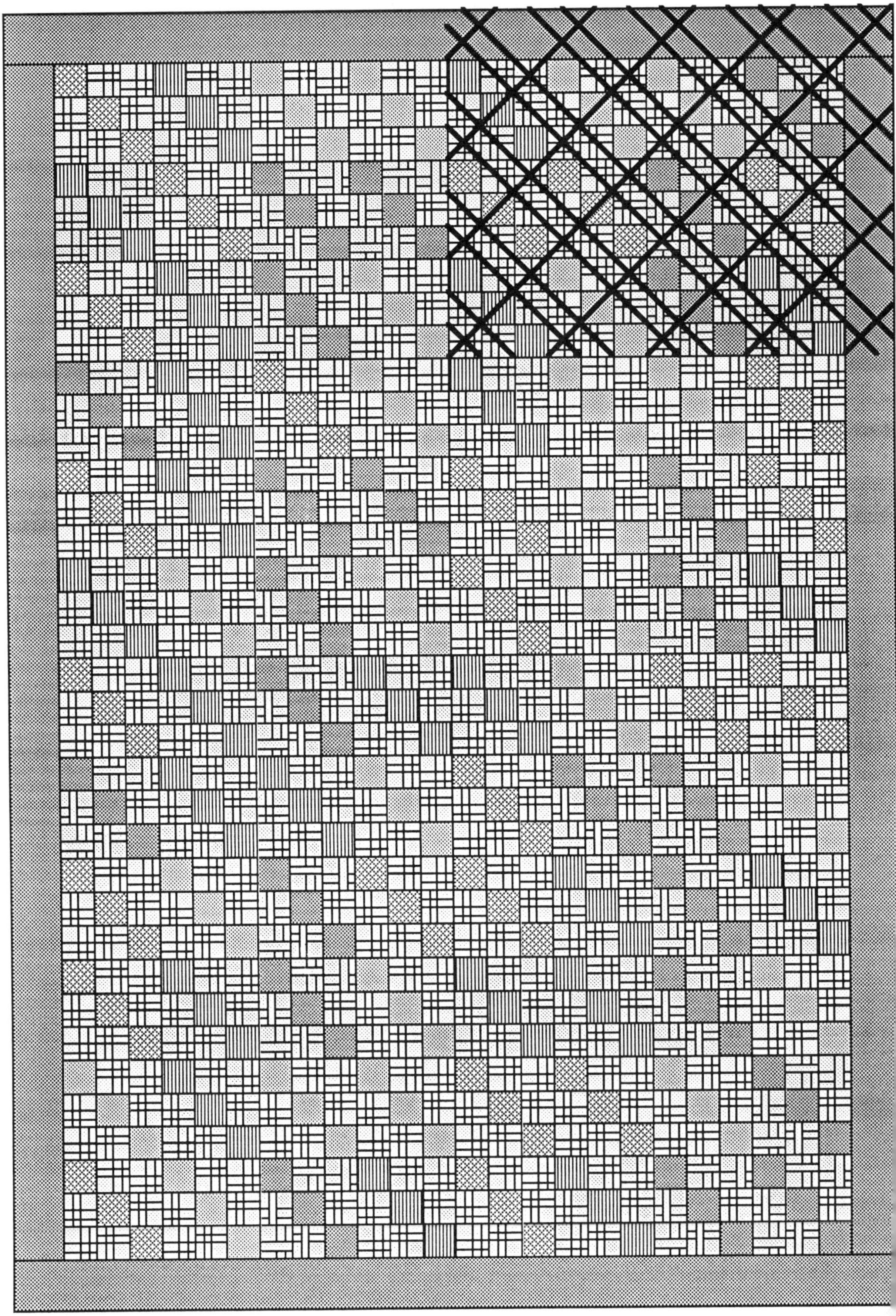

# COUNTRY CHECKS QUILT

Designed and made by Judy Turner

**QUILT INFORMATION (FINISHED SIZES)**
Quilt top, 232 cm x 160 cm
96 Nine-patch blocks, each 18 cm square, and arranged in 12 rows of eight blocks
Border, 8 cm wide

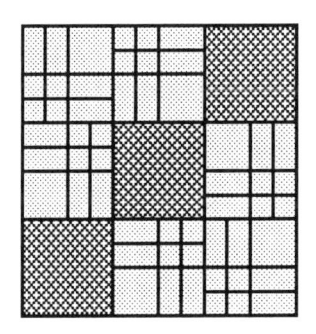

NINE-PATCH BLOCK
Finished size of block, 18 cm square
3 x 3 squares, each 6 cm (finished size)

REQUIREMENTS (112 cm-wide fabric)
3.5 m total assorted light and medium plaids and check fabrics for Nine-patch blocks
1.8 m total assorted dark prints for Nine-patch blocks
2.3 m print for border (or 1.8 m print, with joins to make lengths required)
60 cm check print for binding
240 cm x 170 cm batting
5.2 m backing fabric

## Quilt construction

1. Cut plaids and prints for quilt blocks into 7.5 cm-wide strips, and recut into 7.5 cm squares (see p. 24).
2. Construct Nine-patch blocks (the chain sewing method is appropriate for these blocks — see p. 39). Each block requires six plaid squares and three print squares. Deliberately mismatch the pattern of the plaid and check squares within each block. To add interest, occasionally add one square of a different plaid into a block.
4. Lay out blocks as shown in the quilt plan, balancing colours and tonal values.
5. Sew blocks together (the chain sewing method is appropriate for this quilt — (see p. 46).
6. Cut lengths for border 10 cm wide, joining strips if necessary. Measure quilt through centre to find lengths required.
7. Sew borders to quilt (see p. 49).
8. Prepare backing. Layer quilt top, batting and backing fabric. Quilt by hand or machine (see p. 53). A suggested pattern for the quilting is shown on the quilt plan.
9. Cut strips for binding 6 cm wide. Join strips to make lengths required. Bind quilt (see p. 60).

# BEAR'S PAW QUILT

Designed and made by Beryl Hodges

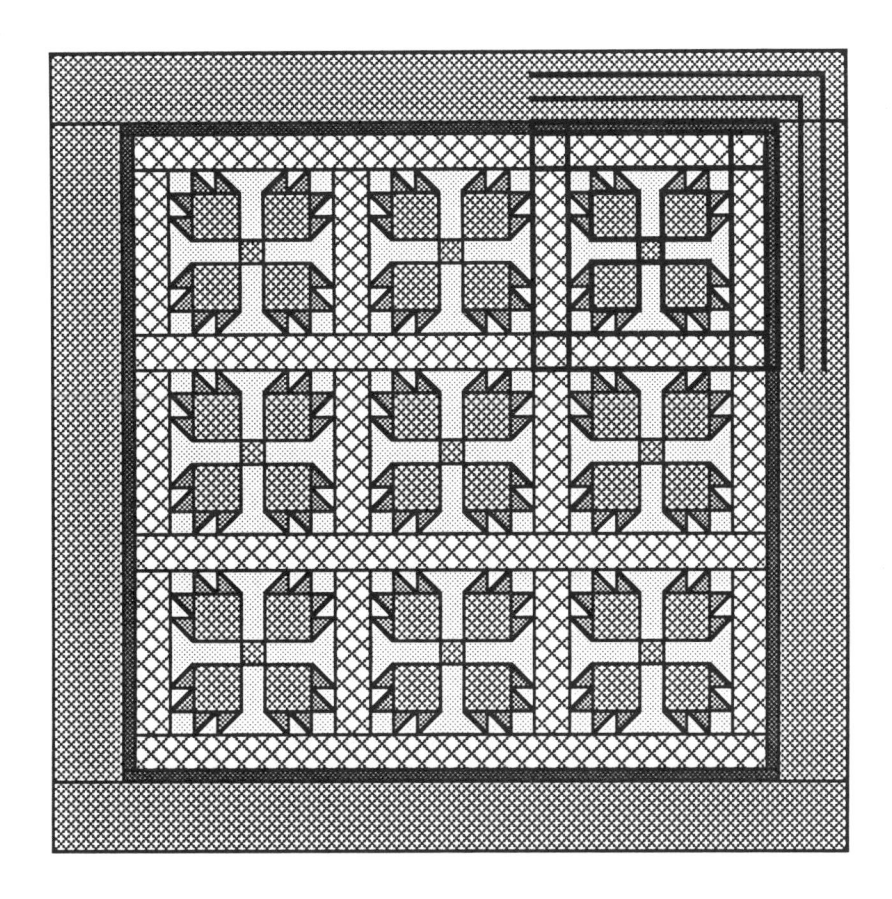

**QUILT INFORMATION (FINISHED SIZES)**
Quilt top, 165 cm x 165 cm
Nine Bear's Paw blocks, each 35 cm square, and arranged in three rows of three blocks
Sashing strips, 7.5 cm wide
Inner border, 3 cm wide
Outer border, 12 cm wide

# METRIC QUILTMAKING

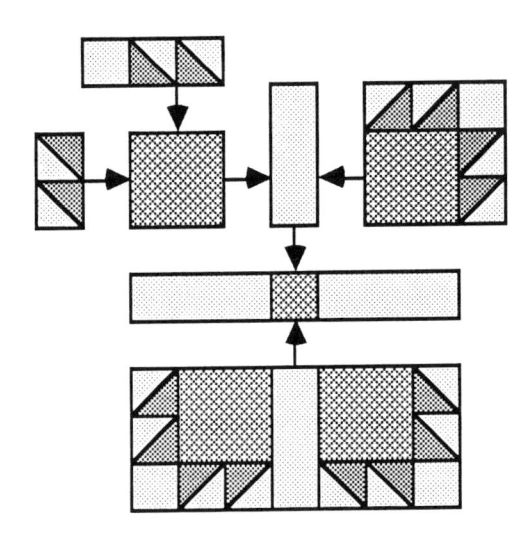

## BEAR'S PAW BLOCK
Finished size of block, 35 cm square
7-patch block, 7 x 7 squares, each 5 cm (finished size)

REQUIREMENTS (112 cm-wide fabric)
1.4 m plaid fabric for outer border
1.4 m check fabric for sashing strips
1.3 m navy and white check for background of Bear's Paw blocks*
1.1 m plain red fabric for inner border and binding
70 cm plain navy fabric for Bear's Paw blocks*
Nine pieces, each 15 cm x 50 cm, assorted red, green and blue plaid fabrics for Bear's Paw blocks
175 cm x 175 cm batting
3.6 m backing fabric
*extra fabric is allowed for the strip-pieced method of making triangle-pieced squares.

### QUILT CONSTRUCTION

1. Make Bear Paw blocks.
From the plain navy and the navy and white check fabrics, make 144 triangle-pieced squares, each cut 6.5 cm x 6.5 cm. Use the strip-pieced half-square triangle technique (see p. 28), and cut the bias strips 6.5 cm wide.
   From navy and white check fabric, cut:
      36 squares, each 6.5 cm x 6.5 cm;
      36 rectangles, each 6.5 cm x 16.5 cm.

From assorted plaid fabrics, and cutting four squares from each plaid, cut 36 squares, each 11.5 cm x 11.5 cm.

Construct Bear's Paw blocks, as shown in diagram for block.

2. From check fabric for sashing, and cutting down the length of the fabric, cut eight strips, each 9 cm wide. Recut four of these strips into 12 lengths, each 9 cm x 36.5 cm. Arrange blocks into three rows of three blocks. Join blocks and short sashing strips into rows, as shown in quilt diagram. Measure the width of the row of blocks and sashing strips, measuring across the centre of the row, and trim remaining four strips to this length. Sew strips to rows of blocks to make centre of the quilt top.

3. From plain red fabric for inner border, cut six strips, each 4.5 cm wide. Join strips to make lengths required as measured through the centre of the quilt, and add strips to quilt top (see p. 49).

4. From plaid fabric for outer border and cutting down the length of the fabric, cut six strips, each 13.5 cm wide. Matching the plaid pattern at joins, join strips as necessary to make the lengths required, remembering to measure through the centre of the quilt. Add border strips to quilt top (see p. 49).

5. Prepare backing fabric. Layer quilt top, batting and backing fabric. Quilt by hand or machine (see p. 53). The dark lines on the quilt plan suggest a quilting pattern.

6. From plain red fabric, cut eight strips for binding, each 8 cm wide. Join strips to make lengths required. Bind quilt (see p. 60).

TO MAKE QUILT LARGER

For quilt 154 cm x 194 cm, make 12 Bear's Paw blocks, and arrange blocks into three rows of four blocks.

**Fabric requirements:** 1.9 m check fabric for sashing; 1.8 m navy and white fabric; 1.7 m plaid fabric for outer border; 1 m plain navy; 1.2 m plain red fabric; 12 pieces plaid fabric, each 15 cm x 50 cm; 164 cm x 204 cm piece of batting; 3.6 m backing.

# LADY OF THE LAKE QUILT

Designed and made by Margaret Rolfe

# QUILT PROJECTS

## QUILT INFORMATION (FINISHED SIZES)
Quilt top, 230 cm x 184 cm
32 Lady of the Lake blocks, each 32.5 cm square, and arranged on the diagonal, as shown.

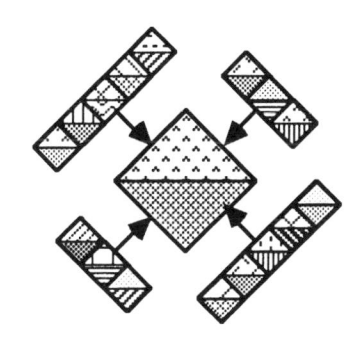

## LADY OF THE LAKE BLOCK
Finished size of block, 32.5 cm square
5-patch block, 5 x 5 squares, each 6.5 cm (finished size)

## REQUIREMENTS (112 cm-wide fabric)
4.5 m total assorted red, blue and combination red and blue prints for the dark side of the Lady of the Lake blocks. Choose a range of shades for each colour, going from rust through to maroons and purple in the reds, and from blue-green through to navy in the blues. Include some hot pink and electric blue as accents.*
4.5 m total assorted beige prints for the light side of the Lady of the Lake blocks*
1.9 m navy print for edge triangles and binding
240 cm x 194 cm batting
4.8 m backing fabric
*extra fabric has been allowed for the strip-pieced method of making triangle-pieced squares.

## QUILT CONSTRUCTION
1. Make Lady of the Lake blocks.
Using the red and blue prints for the dark side, and beige prints for the light side, make 512 triangle-pieced squares, each cut 8 cm x 8 cm. Use the strip-pieced half-square triangle technique (see p. 28), and cut the bias strips 8 cm wide.

From red and blue prints, cut 16 squares, each 22 cm x 22 cm; recut squares on the diagonal to yield 32 half-square triangles.

From beige prints, cut 16 squares, each 22 cm x 22 cm; recut squares on the diagonal to yield 32 half-square triangles.

Construct Lady of the Lake blocks, as shown in diagram for block.

2. From navy print fabric for edge triangles, cut:

7 squares, each 36 cm x 36 cm; re-cut squares across the diagonal to yield 14 half-square triangles;

1 square, 37 cm x 37 cm; recut square across both diagonals to yield four quarter-square triangles.

(Note: these triangles are cut a little larger than required to provide some leeway to cope with any stretching of the bias edges formed.)

3. Lay out blocks as shown in quilt diagram, balancing colours and tonal values. Place large half-square triangles at sides, and quarter-square triangles in the corners. Assemble blocks to make quilt top, following instructions for joining blocks on the diagonal (see p. 45). Trim the edges of the quilt so that all edges are straight and the corners are square (remember to leave the 0.75 cm allowance around the outside when you are trimming the edges). Machine stitch (staystitch) around the edge of the quilt to prevent the bias edges from stretching.

4. Prepare backing fabric. Layer quilt top, batting and backing fabric. Quilt by hand or machine (see p. 53). Quilt in an all-over diagonal grid pattern which follows the piecing, as shown by dark lines on quilt diagram.

5. From navy print for binding, cut nine strips, each 8 cm wide. Join strips together to make lengths required. Bind quilt (see p. 60).

# MARCHING GEESE QUILT

Designed and made by Beryl Hodges

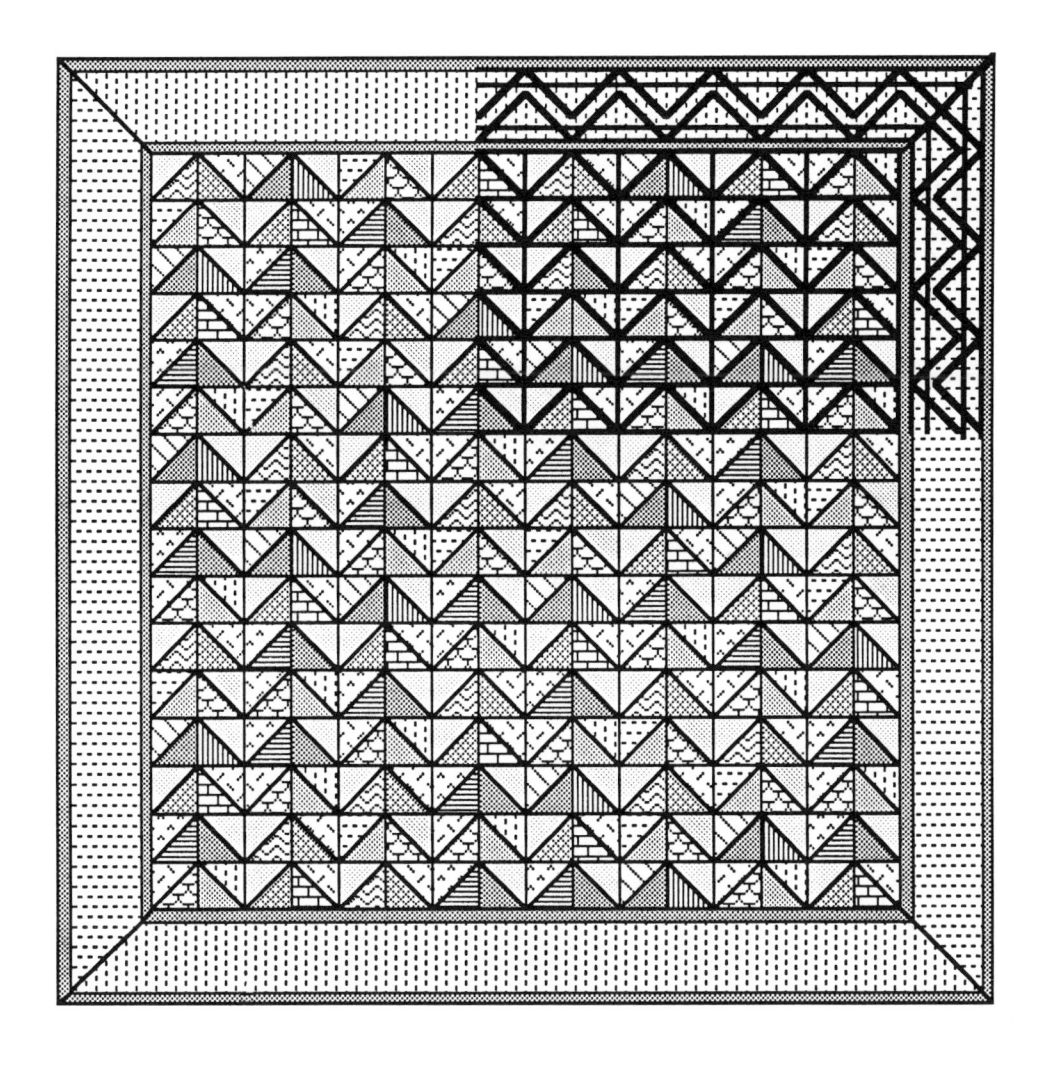

# METRIC QUILTMAKING

### QUILT INFORMATION (FINISHED SIZES)
Quilt top, 122 cm x 122 cm
256 triangle-pieced squares, each 6 cm x 6 cm, and arranged in 16 rows of 16 squares
Border, 13 cm wide (or substitute three borders: a. 2 cm wide; b. 9 cm wide; c. 2 cm wide, as shown in quilt diagram.)

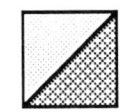

### TRIANGLE-PIECED SQUARE
1-patch triangle design, pieced to make 6 cm x 6 cm square (finished size)

### REQUIREMENTS (112 cm-wide fabric)
1.3 m border print (or substitute 50 cm navy print, and 1.3 m large print)
2 m total assorted beige prints for triangle-pieced squares
70 cm total assorted cherry red prints for triangle-pieced squares
70 cm total assorted green prints for triangle-pieced squares
70 cm total assorted blue prints for triangle-pieced squares
50 cm navy print for binding
132 cm x 132 cm batting
2 m backing fabric

### QUILT CONSTRUCTION
1. Make triangle-pieced squares using the beige (for the background) combined with red, green, and blue prints. Use the strip-pieced half-square triangle technique to make a total of 256 squares, each cut 7.5 cm x 7.5 cm (see p. 28). Cut bias strips 7.5 cm wide.
   Arrange the triangle-pieced squares into the geese pattern as shown, making 16 rows of 16 squares. Join squares into rows, then join rows to make quilt centre.
2. From border print fabric, and cutting down the length of the fabric, cut four strips, each 14.5 cm wide. Following the instructions for making mitred corners (see p. 51), add borders to the centre of the quilt top. (For border print substitute, cut navy print into 3.5 cm strips, joining strips to make required lengths. Cut large print into four strips, each 10.5 cm wide. Join strips of the large print between two navy print strips; use assembled strips instead of the border print.)

# QUILT PROJECTS

3. Prepare backing fabric. Layer quilt top, batting and backing fabric. Quilt by hand or machine (see p. 53). The dark lines on the quilt plan suggest a quilting pattern.

4. From navy print fabric, cut strips for binding 8 cm wide. Join strips to make lengths required. Bind quilt (see p. 60).

TO MAKE QUILT LARGER

For 202 cm x 154 cm quilt, make triangle-pieced squares 8 cm finished size. Cut triangle-pieced squares 9.5 cm x 9.5 cm, cutting bias strips for strip-pieced, half-square triangles 9.5 cm wide. Make 352 squares and arrange in 22 rows of 16 squares.

**Fabric requirements:**

2.1 m border fabric; 4 m total of beige prints; 1.4 m total each of green, cherry and blue prints; 80 cm navy print; 212 cm x 174 cm batting; 3.5 m backing.

# SAILING SHIPS QUILT

Designed and made by Beryl Hodges

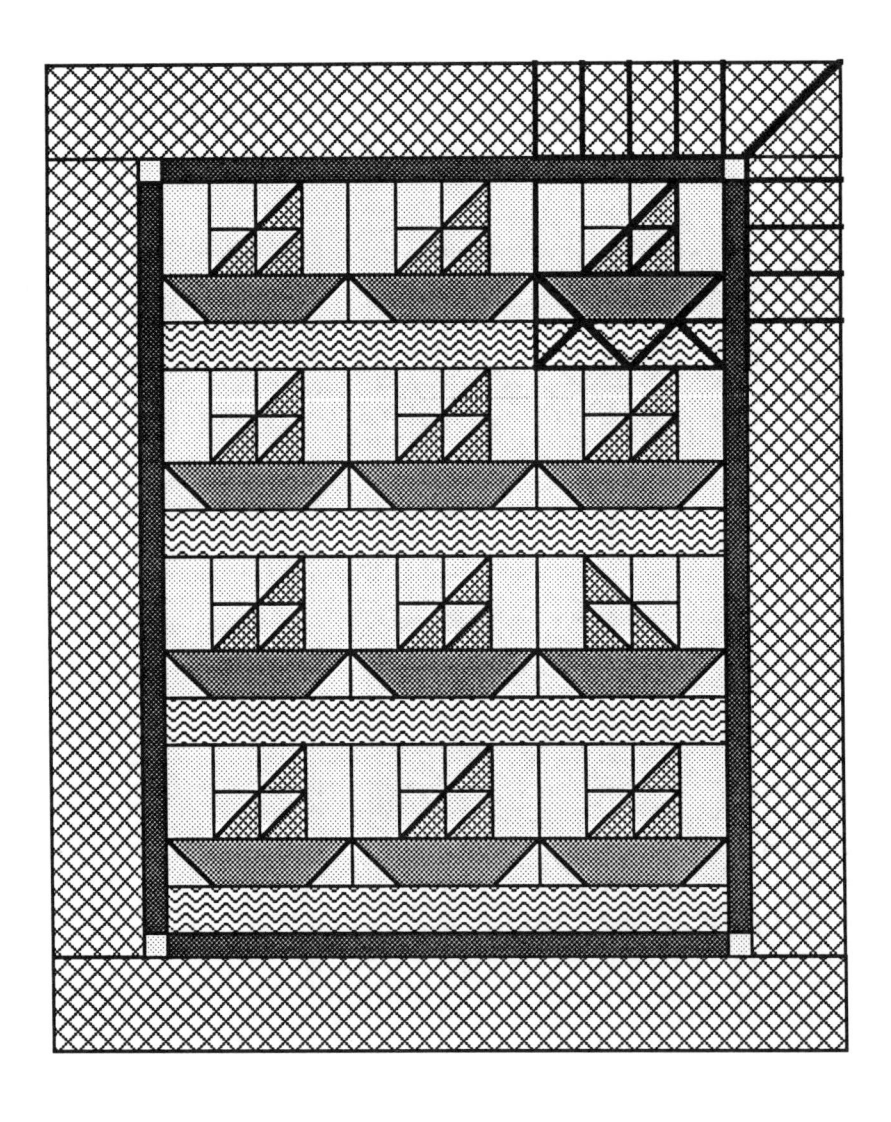

# QUILT PROJECTS

**QUILT INFORMATION (FINISHED SIZES)**
Quilt top, 105 cm x 85 cm
12 Modified Sailing Ship blocks, each 15 cm x 20 cm, arranged in four rows of three blocks
Strips below ships, 5 cm wide
Inner border, 2.5 cm wide, with corner squares
Outer border, 10 cm wide

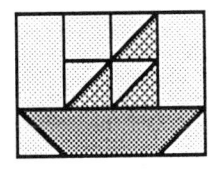

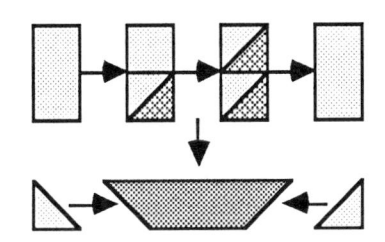

MODIFIED SAILING SHIP BLOCK
Finished size of block, 15 cm x 20 cm
3 x 4 squares, each 5 cm (finished size)

REQUIREMENTS (112 cm-wide fabric)
70 cm striped navy fabric for strips below blocks (extra fabric has been allowed for cutting stripes in right direction)
60 cm plain red fabric for inner border and binding
60 cm navy print for background of Sailing Ship blocks and corner squares of inner border
60 cm plaid fabric for outer border
30 cm total assorted dark plaid and check fabrics for ships' hulls
20 cm total assorted light plaid and check fabrics for ships' sails
115 cm x 95 cm batting
1.2 m backing fabric

**QUILT CONSTRUCTION**

1. Make Sailing Ship blocks.
   From the navy print, cut:
      30 squares, each 7.5 cm x 7.5 cm, then recut across the diagonal to yield 60 half-square triangles;
      12 squares, each 6.5 cm x 6.5 cm;
      24 rectangles, each 6.5 cm x 11.5 cm.
   From the dark plaids, cut 12 rectangles, each 6.5 cm x 13.5 cm. Using a small square ruler, cut each rectangle into the shape for the ship's hull by cutting across the diagonal of each corner.

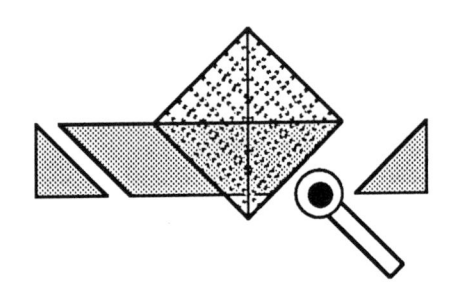

From light plaid fabrics for sails, cut 18 squares each 7.5 cm x 7.5 cm, then cut across diagonal to yield 36 half-square triangles.

Construct Sailing Ship blocks, as shown in diagram for block, remembering to make one block a reverse image.

2. From navy striped fabric, cut four strips, each 6.5 cm x 61.5 cm. Arrange blocks into three rows of four blocks, as shown. Join blocks in rows, then join rows with strips of striped fabric below each row to make quilt centre.

3. From plain red fabric for inner border, cut four strips, each 4 cm wide.

Measure quilt through centre to find border lengths required for both sides and top and bottom strips, measuring only to the edges of the quilt for both lengths. Trim two strips to the correct length for the sides. Trim remaining two strips to correct length for the top and bottom border. Sew side borders in place.

From navy print, cut four squares, each 4 cm x 4 cm. Sew squares to each end of top and bottom border strips, then sew strips to quilt top.

4. From plaid fabric for outer border, cut four strips, each 11.5 cm wide. Add border strips to quilt, measuring quilt through the centre to find lengths required (see p. 49).

5. Prepare backing fabric. Layer quilt top, batting and backing fabric. Quilt by hand or machine (see p. 53). The dark lines on the quilt plan suggest a quilting pattern.

6. From plain red fabric, cut strips for binding 8 cm wide. Join strips to make lengths required. Bind quilt (see p. 60).

# VIBRANT STARS QUILT

Designed and pieced by Margaret Rolfe, quilted by Judy Turner

# METRIC QUILTMAKING

## QUILT INFORMATION (FINISHED SIZES)
Quilt top, 180 cm x 132 cm
24 Evening Star blocks, each 24 cm square, arranged in six rows of four blocks
Inner border, 6 cm wide
Pieced border, 6 cm wide
Outer border, 6 cm wide

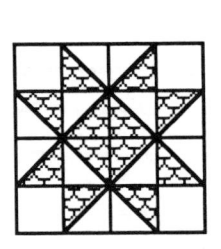

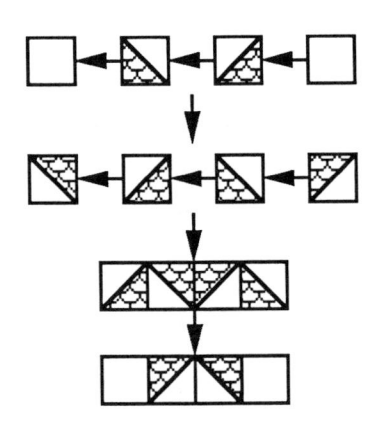

## EVENING STAR BLOCK
Finished size of block, 24 cm square
4-patch block, 4 x 4 squares, each 6 cm (finished size)

## REQUIREMENTS (112 cm-wide fabric)
2 m bright print for Star blocks*
3.7 m plain navy fabric for Star blocks, borders and binding*
190 cm x 142 cm batting
3 m backing fabric
*extra fabric has been allowed for the strip-pieced method of making triangle-pieced squares.

## QUILT CONSTRUCTION
1. From the navy blue fabric, cutting across the width of the fabric, cut a piece 50 cm wide. From remaining approximately 3 m of navy, and cutting down the length of the fabric, cut six strips, each 7.5 cm wide. Set strips aside for borders and binding.
2. Make Evening Star blocks.
Using the bright print and all remaining navy fabric, make 380 triangle-pieced squares, each cut 7.5 cm x 7.5 cm. Use the strip-pieced, half-square triangle technique (see p. 28), and cut the bias strips 7.5 cm wide.
   Construct 24 Evening Star blocks, as shown in the diagram for the block. Remaining

triangle-pieced squares will be used for pieced border.

3. Arrange the blocks in six rows of four blocks each. Sew blocks together to make quilt centre.

4. From the 7.5 cm-wide navy strips, make lengths for borders and binding:
   Using two strips, cut each into two lengths, 190 cm and 109.5 cm respectively.
   Using two strips, cut each into two lengths, 145.5 cm and 140 cm respectively.
   Using two strips, cut each into two lengths, 169.5 cm and 133.5 cm respectively.

5. Sew two navy strips 145.5 cm long, to sides of quilt centre. Sew two navy strips 109.5 cm long to top and bottom of quilt centre.

6. Using remaining pieced squares, and sewing the squares together to make the pattern of the pieced border as shown in quilt diagram, make two lengths each containing 26 triangle-pieced squares, and two lengths each containing 20 triangle-pieced squares. Sew the 26-square lengths to the sides of the quilt, then the 20-square lengths to the top and bottom of the quilt.

7. Using the 169.5 cm lengths, sew strips to sides of quilt for outer border. Sew 133.5 cm lengths to top and bottom.

8. Prepare backing fabric. Layer quilt top, batting and backing fabric. Quilt by hand or machine (see p. 53). Quilt centre of quilt in an all-over diagonal grid pattern which follows the piecing, as shown by dark lines on quilt diagram. Quilt around borders and zigzag around triangles in pieced border.

9. Use remaining navy strips to bind quilt (see p. 60).

TO MAKE QUILT LARGER
For quilt 204 cm x 156 cm, make 11 more Evening Star blocks (35 blocks in all), and arrange blocks in seven rows of five blocks each.
**Fabric requirements:** 3 m brightly coloured print; 5 m plain navy; 214 cm x 166 cm piece of batting; 3.4 m backing fabric.

# OHIO STAR QUILT

Designed and pieced by Margaret Rolfe, quilted by Beth Miller

# QUILT PROJECTS

## QUILT INFORMATION (FINISHED SIZES)
Quilt top, 98 cm x 98 cm
Four Modified Ohio Star blocks, each 30 cm square, and arranged in two rows of two blocks
Inner border, 4 cm wide
Outer border, 15 cm wide

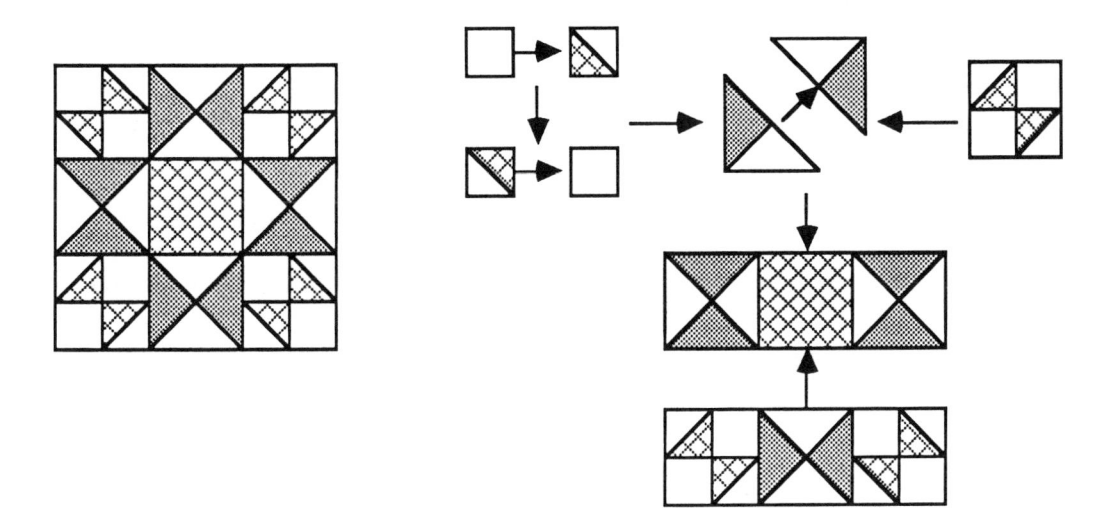

MODIFIED OHIO STAR BLOCK
Finished size of block, 30 cm square
9-patch block, 3 x 3 squares, each 10 cm (finished size)

REQUIREMENTS (112 cm-wide fabric)
1 m border print (or large print) for outer border
90 cm blue print for points of stars, inner border and binding
60 cm white print for background of blocks
30 cm large blue print for centre squares and corner triangles of blocks
108 cm x 108 cm batting
1.1 m backing fabric

## QUILT CONSTRUCTION
1. Make Ohio Star blocks.
    From the white print, cut:
        32 squares, each 6.5 cm x 6.5 cm;
        16 squares, each 7.5 cm x 7.5 cm; recut squares across the diagonal to yield 32 half-square triangles.
        8 squares, each 13.5 cm x 13.5 cm; recut squares across both diagonals to yield 32 quarter-square triangles.

From the large blue print, cut:
  4 squares, each 11.5 cm x 11.5 cm.
  16 squares, each 7.5 cm x 7.5 cm; recut squares across the diagonal to yield 32 half-square triangles.

From the blue print, cut 8 squares, each 13.5 cm x 13.5 cm; recut squares across both diagonals to yield 32 quarter-square triangles.

Construct Ohio Star blocks, as shown in diagram for block.

2. Arrange blocks in two rows of two blocks each. Join blocks into rows, then join rows.
3. From blue print fabric for inner border, cut four strips, each 5.5 cm wide. Following the instructions for adding borders (see p. 49), sew strips to sides and then to top and bottom of quilt top.
4. From border fabric (or large print) for outer border, cut four strips, each 16.5 cm wide. Following the instructions for making borders with mitred corners (see p. 51), add strips to quilt top.
5. Prepare backing fabric. Layer quilt top, batting and backing fabric. Quilt by hand or machine. (see p. 53). Quilting pattern is suggested on one corner of the quilt diagram.
6. From blue print fabric, cut four strips for binding, each 7.5 cm wide. Bind quilt (see p. 60).

TO MAKE QUILT LARGER
For quilt 208 cm x 148 cm, make 11 more Ohio Star blocks (making 15 blocks in all), and arrange blocks into five rows of three blocks. Add an extra 10 cm-wide outer border of the blue print.

**Fabric requirements:** 2 m white print; 2 m border print; 60 cm large blue print; 2.5 m blue print; 158 cm x 218 cm batting; 3.75 m backing.

# CONVERTING IMPERIAL MEASUREMENTS TO METRIC

We are surrounded by wonderful quilting books and magazines coming from America, a country still using the imperial system. In these publications, all the measurements are given in imperial, so you may need help in converting them to metric.

**CONVERTING IMPERIAL MEASUREMENTS**

1. Look at the block design and note two things: first, the measurement of the finished size of the the block; second, how many 'patches' are in the block. Is it a 9-patch, a 4-patch, a 5-patch or a 7-patch? Finding out the number of patches simply means that you work out what grid of squares could be imposed on the block (see p. 63). (This classification of blocks will not cover eight-pointed star blocks, or other blocks which are based on an octagon with eight equal sides, because these are designed from a circle.)

2. Convert the size of the block into metric measurements (see table below), then alter this measurement up or down to the nearest number which is divisible by the number of patches in the block (or, in the case of 9-patch block, a number divisible by 3).

For example, for a 4-patch block which is 12" square, the nearest equivalent will be either 30 cm or 32 cm. As 32 is divided more neatly by four than 30 cm, you may choose to make the block this size. Then each patch will be 8 cm finished size. Thus, squares for the block would be cut 9.5 cm square, half-square triangles would be cut from 10.5 cm squares, and quarter-square triangles from 11.5 cm squares.

If the 12" block were a 9-patch, then 30 cm would be chosen as the size (because 30 cm is divided neatly by three). Each patch in the block would be 10 cm-square finished size, so squares would be cut 11.5 cm square, half-square triangles would be cut from 12.5 cm squares and quarter-square triangles from 13.5 cm squares.

If you were trying to combine 4-patch and 9-patch blocks in the one quilt, opt for the 30 cm size, because this is the most convenient for the 9-patch block. For the 30 cm 4-patch block, the finished size of the patches would be 7.5 cm square. Squares would then be cut 9 cm, half-square triangles from 10 cm squares, and quarter-square triangles from 11 cm squares.

Another example is a 5-patch block which measures 12½". The nearest metric equivalent for the size of the block is either 30 cm or 35 cm (the nearest actual metric equivalent of 12½" is 32 cm, but this does not divide neatly by five). If you choose the 30 cm block, the size of the finished patches would be 6 cm, so squares would be cut 7.5 cm square, half-square triangles would be cut from 8.5 cm squares and quarter-square triangles from 9.5 cm squares. If you choose the 35 cm block, the size of the finished squares would be 7 cm, so squares would be cut 8.5 cm square, half-square triangles would be cut from 9.5 cm squares and quarter-square triangles from 10.5 cm squares.

Alternatively, the process of conversion could be reversed by finding the size of the patches in the block, converting this size to a metric measurement, then multiplying this measurement by the number of patches to give the block size. For example, the 4-patch 12" block has patches which are 3". The metric equivalent for 3" is 8 cm, so 8 cm is the size of the finished patches. Multiply this by the number of patches in the block, which is four, and this gives you the size of the block in a metric measurement — 32 cm.

The reason for working out the sizes this way is that it results in manageable figures. It is pointless to take a block size, convert it to its nearest metric measurement, and then find this measurement will not divide neatly into the size you need for the number of patches in the block.

#### METRIC EQUIVALENTS

Below is a list of useful metric equivalents for imperial measurements to be used for patchwork. Note that they are not exact equivalents. For some measurements, alternatives are given, so choose the size which is most appropriate for the block you are making.

¼" = 0.75 cm

½" = 1 cm, or 1.5 cm when adding two 0.75 seam allowances together

¾" = 2 cm

1" = 2.5 cm

1¼" = 3 cm

1½" = 4 cm

2" = 5 cm

2½" = 6 cm

# CONVERTING IMPERIAL MEASUREMENTS TO METRIC

3" = 8 cm
4" = 10 cm
5" = 12 cm
6" = 15 cm, or 16 cm
8" = 20 cm
9" = ¼ yd = 24 cm
10" = 24 cm (for 9-patch or 4-patch blocks) or 25 cm (for 5-patch blocks)
12" = 30 cm (for 9-patch, 4-patch and 5-patch blocks), or 32 cm (for 4-patch blocks, particularly those which have divisions within the patches)
14" = 36 cm (for 4-patch blocks), or 35 cm (for 7-patch blocks)
15" = 36 cm (for 9-patch and 4-patch blocks) or 35 cm (for 5-patch blocks)
16" = 40 cm
18" = ½ yd = 45 cm, or 48 cm
20" = 50 cm
36" = 1 yd = 90 cm
40" = 100 cm
44" = 112 cm

# INDEX:
## PATCHWORK AND BLOCK DESIGNS

1-patch 66, 78—79
4-patch 65, 86—98
5-patch 65, 98—102
7-patch 66, 102—104
9-patch 64—65, 80—85

Anvil 93
Autumn Leaves 104
Barn raising arrangement 79
Baskct 85
Bear's Paw 103, 112
Birds in the Air (9-patch) 83
Birds in the Air (4-patch) 96
Brick pattern 79
Buckeye Beauty 68, 88
Cake Stand 102
Chequer Board 79
Churn Dash 83
Diamond Star 98
Double Wrench 99
Double X (9-patch) 82
Double X (4-patch) 67, 97
Duck and Ducklings 99
Dutchman's Puzzle 91
Evening Star 89, 124
Flower Basket 92
Flying Geese 101
Flying Geese arrangement 79, 118
Four-patch 86
Four X Star 100

Hen and Chickens 103
Indian Star 89
Jacob's Ladder 85
Kansas Troubles 92
Lady of the Lake 101, 115
Maple Leaf 84
Milky Way 82
Mosaic 96
Nine-patch 80, 109
Ocean Waves 94
Ohio Star 84, 127
Old Maid's Puzzle 90
Pinwheel 86
Puss in the Corner 94
Rail fence 79
Road to Oklahoma 90
Sailing Ship 95, 121
Sawtooth Star 67, 88
Shoo-Fly 81
Split Nine-patch 81, 106
Trip Around the World 79
Wedding Ring 100
Whirligig 87
Yankee Puzzle 87